To Dee Dee

In Times
Like These

Malcolm Boyd

In Times Like These

How We Pray

MALCOLM BOYD & J. JON BRUNO
EDITORS

SEABURY BOOKS
an imprint of
CHURCH PUBLISHING, NEW YORK

A catalog record for this book is available from
the Library of Congress.

ISBN: 1-59627-015-2

Church Publishing Incorporated
445 Fifth Avenue
New York, NY 10016
www.churchpublishing.org

5 4 3 2 1

To
Mary Bruno
and
Mark Thompson

Contents

ACKNOWLEDGMENTS   15

INTRODUCTION
     Malcolm Boyd   17

PRAYER BEADS IN IRAQ
     *A military chaplain finds his prayer life deepened
     in unexpected ways.*
          Frank E. Wismer III   29

BRINGING FORTH BUDDHA NATURE
     A Buddhist priest describes Zen prayer.
          Catherine Toldi   35

PRAYER IN A DARK TIME
     *One man's prayerful vision of a helping hand across
     the cold, raging waters of addiction . . .*
          Brian Gleason   42

PRAYER A LA CUCINA
     *A favorite prayer from the kitchen . . . good, hearty,
     earthy soup.*
          Lauri D. Goldenhersh   48

I FEEL PRAYER IS MUCH ABUSED
     A literary and cultural icon talks about prayer.
          Norman Mailer   52

PRESENCE OF THE HOLY
*Through prayer, a law enforcement officer who kills a
man in the line of duty eventually finds wholeness and
another way in which to serve . . . as a bishop of the
church.*
            J. Jon Bruno   54

GOD, KEEP ME IN THE MUSIC
*Through writing music, a composer slowly wakes up
to a prayerful spirituality. . . .*
            David Avshalomov   57

O THOU! O THOU!
*A much-loved American writer describes his
prayer life.*
            Frederick Buechner   62

PRAYER IN CITY HALL
A hardened reporter's prayers of intercession.
            Marc B. Haefele   64

LAUGHING WITH GOD
A playwright offers up humor as a prayerful activity.
            Felix Racelis   72

CAN A FILM BE A PRAYER?
A filmmaker says, "Absolutely."
            Stephen Vittoria   76

Praying in Between
*The author of celebrated spirituality titles writes candidly
about fretting through prayerful silences....*
Nora Gallagher 85

In the Dry Arroyos of the Badlands
A Lakota way of prayer.
Robert W. Two Bulls 89

How I Pray
*An elder statesman of religion in America offers a
meditation upon prayer — both informal and formal.*
Martin E. Marty 94

¡Qué lista la Virgen!
*An advocate for the poor offers the prayerful example
of the Virgin of Guadalupe.*
Lydia Lopez 99

The Day the Tank Arrived
*A journalist who covers our "hurt and broken world"
reports on prayer and the power of the pen.*
Pat McCaughan 104

In a Hospice
*A hospice nurse writes about prayer from a privileged
perspective.*
Laura Treister 110

THE ANNIVERSARY OF KAREN'S DEATH
  A husband's prayerful good-bye to his wife.
      Chester Talton   113

WHY DO I GO TO CHURCH FIVE TIMES A DAY?
  Communal prayer in a religious community.
      Sister Cintra Pemberton, OSH   117

IF PRAYER IS A THREAD
  A distinguished novelist writes with candor and force
  about his relationship with God.
      Felice Picano   123

PRAYER IN ISLAM
  A female Muslim physician describes the riches of prayer
  practice in her faith.
      Laila Al-Marayati   130

FINALLY LETTING HER DIE
  Through prayer, a father confronts the sudden death
  of a daughter.
      James A. Hoyal   135

A SUPERNATURAL BATTLE
  A woman prays "like a house afire" for release
  from the demons of mental illness, alcohol, and
  drugs.
      Tory Connolly Walker   139

An Immigrant in America Prays
  Prayer is something this Sri Lankan immigrant is still
  trying to sort out.
        Ravi GuneWardena   144

Confessions of an AIDS Activist
  A worker for the World Health Organization ruminates
  on prayer, hope . . . and helplessness.
        Ted Karpf   148

Side Doors Opening
  A lecturer, author, and authority on religion in America
  parses the relationship between creativity and prayer.
        Phyllis Tickle   152

To Perform with Leonard Bernstein
  A professional musician explains why Carnegie Hall
  is a fine place to pray.
        Norm Freeman   156

A Red Rose over My Chest
  A cabaret performer offers a novel view of the prayer-
  ful life.
        Joseph "Go" Mahan   163

Prison Prayers
  A jailed husband and his wife pray.
        Mark Peavey and
        Lynne Dunnington Peavey   166

HAVE MIND AND BODY HEALED?
  A prayer story from the Oklahoma City bombing.
      Susan Urbach   172

WRITING ICONS
  An icon painter's approach to prayer
      Sister Ellen Francis, OSH   176

THE ART OF BEING HUMAN ON A FULL-TIME BASIS
  *Prayer, for the dean of a great cathedral, is about
  showing up for one's own life.*
      Alan Jones   179

WHY AREN'T I MY FATHER'S SON?
  *A National Public Radio commentator and sportswriter's
  prayer life.*
      Frank Deford   184

MOTHER BROKE HER HIP
  *A son learns humble prayer lessons from tending to
  an elderly, incapacitated parent.*
      Malcolm Boyd   187

THE JUNG GROUP IN A SYNAGOGUE
  *A psychotherapist reaches for help beyond
  psychotherapy. . . .*
      Nan C. Gold   191

WRITER'S BLOCK OR ARTIST'S BLOCK
A professional illustrator draws the line on prayer.
Steve Ross   196

A CLEARER PICTURE
For this theater and television actor, it's all prayer.
Jeff Allin   200

THANK YOU
A mother's prayer of thanksgiving for her gay son.
Jane Tully   202

FOLLOWING THE BREADCRUMBS
*A professional photographer takes photographs of
remnants of meals — and discovers that our times of
fellowship together are emblems of prayers prayed.*
Cynthia Rush   204

THREE PRAYERS FROM A YOUNG ADULT WEEKEND
Spencer Smilanick, Tinia Orduña,
and Holly Martin   208

PRAYER IN A HOSPITAL
*A hospital chaplain understands prayer as an attitude,
a way of being.*
Gretchen Haight   213

HOW I PRAYED ON 9/11
A prayerful first response to a suffering city on 9/11.
Debra A. Wagner   217

14 *Contents*

IT TAKES A MOUNTAIN OR AN OCEAN
A modern-day Thoreau recommends us to the spiritual tutelage of mountaintops.
Michael Seiler 223

PRAYER ON THE STREETS
A priest learns to pray in the in-between places of her life.
Anna B. Olson 230

LISTENING
A spirituality workshop leader and author highlights the prayerful qualities of listening.
Kay Lindahl 239

T-CELLS AND EMPATHY
A seasoned therapist and author makes prayer real... with the help of two remarkable friends.
Mark Thompson 244

THE SEASONS TUMBLE
An acclaimed author, thinker, and educator drifts a bit — ecumenically — when he prays.
Harvey Cox 251

Acknowledgments

W E THANK Johnny R. Ross for his vision, skill, hard work, imagination, good humor, and extraordinary commitment in the realization of this book. His gift is an incalculable one. Lauri D. Goldenhersh contributed endless hours and patience, sound counsel, communications skills with contributors, and always a deep sense of perspective. Our gratitude is also extended to a number of people whose assistance was instrumental in bringing the book to completion, including Dr. Gwynne Guibord, Gretchen Haight, Mark E. Asman, and Michael Cooper. Finally, our sincere and warm thanks to a splendid group of contributors.

Introduction

PRAYER, in all its complexity and simplicity, embraces differences and similarities, body and soul, sacred and secular, mystery and ordinariness. All these are reflected in the various prayer lives, experiences, and histories that follow in the pages of this book.

Of course, my prayers have been deeply affected over the years by events that shaped our world — and, on a very personal level, my own life. Yet personal prayer is not part of the memory of my early years, despite the fact I sang as a boy in a parish choir, was a youthful acolyte serving at an altar, and discovered there was plenty to pray about in my family. We were well-to-do, even privileged, but there was also a lot of violence, pain, insecurity, and fear.

Later, in my twenties when I worked in Hollywood in the motion picture industry and early television, I was respectful of religion but stayed distanced from it. Seemingly I could only bring my intellect to it, not my heart. I was fascinated by the church's magnificent liturgy and music. However, I was like the rich young ruler in the New Testament; I wasn't about to surrender my sovereignty or make a commitment.

At twenty, I wanted to be a millionaire. Glamour beckoned. I was willing to take virtually any risk for success. Meanwhile, the question of meaning gnawed at my insides. I was aware of it as terribly important, but somehow beyond my reach. Yet I started searching, very quietly and methodically. On early Sunday mornings I visited different churches. Always I sat in a back row, avoided contact with people (especially a priest), and slipped outside during the singing of the last hymn. I didn't want to get involved. Heaven forbid.

This kind of religious ritual in my life continued over an extended period of time. Then, to my utter surprise, I found myself sitting in a bishop's office one day. I thought I had made the appointment just to get a little help with this search of mine, which wasn't really going very well. However, before I left the bishop's office that day, I had asked to become a postulant for holy orders — to become a priest in the Episcopal Church.

What had happened? I had started to pray.

This was seemingly for the first time in my life. At least seriously. I became aware that prayer changes the person who is praying. I was tearing down walls separating me from life. I began to open up my life to God, other people, circumstances, situations, challenges, new things. It was an extraordinary feeling. Shedding my skin. Seeing with fresh eyes. Perceiving whole new worlds. I was in awe. It occurred to me that I no longer belonged simply to myself. In some mysterious way I didn't exactly understand, I belonged to God.

At thirty, I had departed Hollywood, was in the midst of six years of theological training, and the world I previously knew had been turned upside down. Now prayer was at the center of things. I spent a lot of time examining my motives about everything, often feeling a total failure or an absolute fool. In the face of holiness, I said (and desperately meant), "I am not worthy."

I prayed with fervor. Could I rid myself of narcissism? No. I couldn't seem to do anything by my own strength. Yet I knew God could heal me. Everything was endlessly strung out to dry in my mind. At times I felt like a medievalist who pondered angelology. In seminary my Old Testament class was at 8:00 a.m. I couldn't keep my eyes open; the professor's voice droned on. Hurry, I mustn't miss a beat, a new thought, a fresh fact. Church History followed; we seemed to cover a hundred years in a single hour. New Testament. Liturgics. Theology.

And, here is prayer again: "Almighty God, to you all hearts are open, all desires known, and from you no secrets are hid: Cleanse the thoughts of our hearts by the inspiration of your Holy Spirit, that we may perfectly love you, and worthily magnify your holy Name; through Christ our Lord. Amen."

No secrets. I am naked, exposed. How can I perfectly love God when I don't seem to know what love is, in the first place, and certainly don't love most other people — and clearly don't love (or remotely understand) myself? God, will you teach me? Transform me? Mold me? Breathe new life into my soul?

There were occasions when it became clear to me I was praying in a hypocritical way. Here's an example. I was saying the Lord's Prayer: "Forgive us our sins as we forgive those who sin against us." But I hadn't. I knew it, instinctively and quickly. I saw myself as a phony, a spiritual poseur, and — on top of all that — I was lying to God: literally praying to God for forgiveness when I knowingly denied it to someone else. I had homework to do.

Something remarkable happened to my prayer life when I spent time in the Taizé Community of France in 1957. Up to that time my prayer was very interiorly directed and concerned with (like Mama Rose in *Gypsy*) ME — ME — ME. Taizé is an ecumenical monastic community in a small rural village in Burgundy. Taizé taught me that the presence of Jesus Christ in the world — the simple presence — cannot be without effect. So it's understood that the life of all Christians can be seen as the life of Jesus Christ within them. I discovered a new sense of movement in a Christian style of life: Jesus runs, joyously and lovingly, to meet us in the world. Our response involves our running toward Jesus. My experience at Taizé opened my consciousness about a lot of things: servanthood in the world, issues of justice and peace, ecumenism, and how strategic, patient, unpublicized penetration of culture can be evangelism of the highest order. The running imagery — both of Jesus and of a responsive style of life — influenced me deeply when I later wrote my book of prayers, *Are You Running with Me, Jesus?*

At forty, I'd served an inner-city parish in Indianapolis and a college chaplaincy in Colorado, gone on a Prayer Pilgrimage–Freedom Ride in 1961, embraced the civil rights struggle, and was presently a chaplain at Wayne State University in Detroit. On the Freedom Ride I joined a number of other Episcopal priests, black and white. I recall one of them remarked, "It seems to me this is really a kind of prayer — a corporate confession of sin."

In the 1970s, when I turned fifty, two big issues confronted the church. One was the question of whether to ordain women. The debate was particularly heated in the Episcopal Church, which was why *Ms.* magazine asked me to write a cover story entitled "Who's Afraid of Women Priests — And Why Are They Afraid?" But the issue forced the whole religious world to reexamine ideas of ordained identity and, by extension, ideas of identity in general. For example: homosexual identity. Should gay men and lesbians be welcomed into church? Ordained as priests? Have their unions blessed? Would others in the church receive them as equals and offer love? This issue battered my own reality: I was a gay man who had not yet felt it was possible to come out. If I did, could my ministry continue? Would I be acceptable?

This provoked an extraordinary prayer crisis in my life. I felt a lot of anger. Hadn't organized religion, including the church, long persecuted gay people and refused to offer unconditional love? Indeed, was it possible for me to pray through my pain and rage? Trying to be quite realistic, could I offer unconditional love to the church? There was another aspect, too. My self-esteem as a person (a gift from God in creation) had been battered cruelly by the church's seeming rejection. Could I find a lifeline in prayer to discover healing in Christ's love?

Later, when I began to wonder "how" it might be possible for me to come out, I wrote confidentially to a friend who was the editor of a national magazine asking for advice. But, when it came, it was unsettling and not helpful. She believed that being identified as a gay man would "destroy my effectiveness" in Christian ministry (she wrote me in a letter) and — even more ominously — would lead to "my crucifixion."

Four years later when I came out, I identified in a sense with a character (portrayed by actor Jack Nicholson) in Antonioni's film *The Passenger*. This man assumes the identity of a dead man whom he happens to resemble physically. Now he has a new passport, a new identity, even a new skin. He has become someone else whom he does not know at all.

It is a curious experience that carries him into new relationships and experiences — and ultimately to his death. The film resonated with me because, after coming out, I moved on unfamiliar ground. I moved through intricate new phases and steps. Sometimes I wasn't sure where I was going, and I discovered a number of people no longer responded to "me" but to an image that I felt was quite like a stranger.

Healing and wholeness followed slowly and gradually. I found self-worth is a gift of God. It took a while for this to permeate my consciousness. I did not have to earn it (as if I could anyhow) but had only to accept it with gratitude.

When I celebrated my sixtieth birthday in 1983, I was on the staff at St. Augustine by-the-Sea parish in Santa Monica, California. My prayer life increasingly reflected the world I lived in, the people I saw or knew, and different ways I reacted to my environment. The plague of AIDS was a large part of this reality. I remember one young man who told me in a hospital about his night sweats, chills and fever, and diarrhea, but also about his faith, his goal to have "a wonderful, beautiful death," and anticipation to hang out with Jesus in an afterlife. Another young man asked me to meet him inside the church. Removing his shoes, socks, and shirt, he invited me to anoint with oil the soles of his feet, his chest, and the palms of his hands. He asked for the administration of the last rites because he wished to deal fully with death several months prior to his departure from this life. His intention was to live the rest of his life in the freedom of resurrection. These spiritual experiences, and examples of faith, shook up any lethargy that might have crept into my life.

My eightieth birthday loomed up in 2003. Through all my years I've been struck by the spiritual accuracy of these words from theologian Karl Barth: "There is suffering and sinking, a being lost and a being rent asunder, in the peace of God." His words touched me anew as I contemplated the question: what is the purpose of the rest of my life?

The question seems presumptuous and self-serving against the backdrop of the world's agonies and tragedies. Yet I find it a demanding one. I must ask it because — as I look at the end of my life — my inadequacies and failures bluntly confront me. My grotesquely obvious failures to fully love God and other people. The lesson this teaches me is: my faith depends so completely on the strength of God's grace. The integrity and power of my prayer come from God, not me. I am a pilgrim, not a role model. Seeking a clear path to God, often I tend to get in my own way, stumble, and veer off the course. Yet, at the same time, I realize the immediate grace of being saved and nurtured; welcomed again and again as a prodigal; freely given the opportunity — again! — to choose life.

I pray now far more than I used to do. In all sorts of moments, places, and ways. Proper, formal ones. Improper, informal ones. Prayer can take the form of a conversation; be nonverbal; occur in the presence of a loved person or

animal or tree, a bright early morning or a dark night. I pray
for those who anger me, and get over my anger. I pray in the
throes of envy, and am able to laugh at my own absurdity.
I pray daily for those who have died, and now they live
in my consciousness. I try to pray positively rather than
negatively, seeking wholeness over fragmentation, healing
over hand-wringing.

Approaching the end of my life, and a continuing journey
into God's eternity, my prayer is one of enormous gratitude.

— MALCOLM BOYD

In Times
Like These

Prayer Beads in Iraq

Frank E. Wismer III

*A military chaplain finds his prayer life deepened
in unexpected ways.*

WE WERE in the midst of our early morning worship at Saddam Hussein's former presidential palace in Baghdad, Iraq, when a huge explosion rocked the entire structure. As the chaplain for the Coalition Provisional Authority, I was leading the prayers but opened my eyes for a moment to see the entire congregation cringing in expectation that the ceiling might come crashing down at any moment. I simply closed my eyes again and continued. Later I would learn that the blast had occurred a mile away, and twenty-three people had been murdered at the so-called Assassins' Gate checkpoint leading into the Green Zone. (The Assassins' Gate was so named months before when Iraqi Republican Guard troops used it as a sniper position.) I would also learn later that one of the Iraqi day workers who regularly worshiped with us at the 10:30 a.m. service had perished in the explosion. She had been trapped in a vehicle near the suicide bomber's car and was incinerated when the heat of the blast welded the doors closed, preventing her from escaping.

Hadeel was a lovely twenty-five-year-old who worked as a linguist for the Coalition. Her personality and smile were infectious, and she was popular with both the Iraqis and Americans who worked in the palace. She was also engaged to be married. Just the day before, Hadeel had been in our chapel to attend the memorial service of her friend Nahla Waheed. Nahla was a young Muslim woman who had been killed when the vehicle in which she was traveling was struck by an improvised explosive device (IED). She had been seated in the rear of the vehicle between two soldiers. Neither of them had received a scratch, but she had died from the shrapnel.

One of the rules by which I attempt to live is, "I desire to be a nonanxious presence in the world." This rule sounds great on the surface, but just try living by it — especially when, at any moment, you might instantly be blown up by a passing car or maimed by an incoming mortar shell. To live as a nonanxious presence in the world was easy when I was dwelling in the safety of my home or the secure environment of my community. But living under the constant threat of violence and danger required me to undertake an intentional approach to conducting myself as a nonanxious presence in the world. How would I live with serenity in the midst of continual danger?

In 1998 while I was serving with the NATO peacekeeping forces in Bosnia, our Civil Affairs team was tasked to visit the Turkish Brigade in Zenica to conduct a short course in Civil-Military Cooperation (CIMIC) on behalf of Multi-National Division North. Toward the end of our stay with the Turks, they invited us to tour the historic city of Travnik that served as the capital of Bosnia during the Ottoman Empire. While in Travnik, we visited and toured a seventeenth-century mosque. As we were escorted through the prayer area, I spied a basket that was filled with sets of prayer beads that appeared similar to Christian rosaries. My curiosity got the best of me, and I inquired about them. I was informed that they were, in fact, prayer beads and that they were used during worship and private prayer. I was also instructed that these strands of beads contain thirty-three each, representing the years of Jesus' life. I was intrigued and determined to obtain a set of Islamic prayer beads to begin using in my private devotions.

It was the Mufti in Tuzla, Bosnia, near Eagle Base where I was stationed who taught me how to pray the beads, using this mantra: "God is Great. God is One. Praise be to God the Master of the Universe." Upon my return from Bosnia, the prayer beads I had acquired found a home in my car. I keep them around the gearshift. I have them there because I have discovered that while driving I do not conduct myself as a nonanxious presence in the world. As a matter of fact, it is while driving that I am easily transformed into a raging maniac. I wondered if the prayer beads might help me on the road. What I have discovered is truly amazing. If I begin my travels by praying, I can be calm and serene. If I use them when someone swerves into my lane or races up behind me, my countenance remains peaceful. The beads and mantra still my fears and calm my soul.

The prayer in Arabic, which I learned in Iraq, begins, "Subhan Allah." Allah is, of course, the Arabic word for God used by Muslims, Jews, and Christians alike. Subhan is a little more difficult to explain. It is a word that defies definition. God is always more than our ability to comprehend or explain. God always surpasses our finite ability to grasp. Therefore, the word "Subhan" is a word that cannot quite be explained. God is Great, but God is more than that. Subhan captures the essence of the incomprehensibility of God. Equally incomprehensible to me is the way in which praying this mantra restores my equilibrium, my centeredness, and my serenity.

It is commonplace in Iraq to see men carrying their prayer beads with them wherever they go. It is the rule rather than the exception to see Muslim men praying in public not only during prayer time but also throughout the day while fingering their beads. One man will be seen praying at a bus stop. Another will be walking through the market while privately praising Allah with his prayer beads.

The longer I stayed in Iraq, the more profound an impression men praying made upon me. I was surrounded with a faithful community of Muslim men who were praying continually. It dawned on me that if I were to live as a nonanxious presence in the world, I would have to center my life in prayer. So, I got into the habit of carrying my prayer beads with me wherever I went. I would pray walking down the street. I would pray as I waited for a meeting to begin. I would pray while traveling in a convoy. I remember that on one convoy the window of the vehicle in which I was riding was struck with a rock thrown in anger by a teenage boy. I saw him as he hurled it at me. Wondering how to respond to this assault, I simply lifted up my hand with the prayer beads I'd been praying and mouthed the words for him to see, "Subhan Allah. Hamdu Allah. La Elah Ela Allah...." I was at peace and serene; my enemy was not.

Many years ago, prayer was described to me as a lever able to lift what would otherwise be too heavy for me. My first impression of this metaphor was that prayer could be used as leverage to move God. Since then, I have, indeed, discovered that prayer is a lever. But it isn't God who is moved by the lever that is prayer. I am the one who is moved! When my burdens are too heavy or my problems seem too overwhelming, prayer is able to lift me. Prayer restores my peace and sanity and serenity. Prayer restores me to calm in the midst of chaos. Prayer permits me to live out my rule of life. And it is as I live out my rule of life that I am at one with myself and with others and reacquainted with God.

God is Great.

God is One.

Praise be to God (who is) the Master of the Universe.

Bringing Forth Buddha Nature

CATHERINE TOLDI

A Buddhist priest describes Zen prayer.

IT WAS PAST MIDNIGHT, and he had still not returned. I lay in the back of the truck, my heart pounding with fear. My life companion was climbing his first "big wall," the Direct North Buttress, a two-thousand-foot-high granite cliff that rises from the Yosemite valley floor. He and his climbing partner had left at dawn, saying they expected to return by nightfall. That was eighteen hours ago.

Thankfully, I wasn't alone. A friend had come along. Earlier that evening, we'd talked with a climber at the village store (we called him "our angel") who told us, "Oh, Direct North Buttress, it's notorious for people getting off route. It's so complex. People often have to sleep up top. I wouldn't even begin to worry until the morning."

Okay. I'll try not to worry "until the morning." So my friend and I lay side by side in our sleeping bags, waiting. Breathing in, and breathing out. For hours. I tried to reassure myself, repeating the words of our angel. I kept telling myself, *I know they will be safe. Somehow.* But each passing moment seemed to peel off another layer of my self. I could no longer bear to think my thoughts. I surrendered my mind to the raw, empty feeling. And out of the silence, the words welled up: *Kanzeon, na mu butsu yo butsu u in yo butsu u en . . .* — the Buddhist invocation to Kanzeon, the enlightening being of compassion. The "one who hears the cries of the world."

. . . bup po so en jo raku ga jo cho nen Kanzeon bo nen Kanzeon nen nen ju shin ki nen nen fu ri shin . . . repeating the words, I began to relax. My pulse slowed down, extended out into the night. I felt the presence of my lover like a luminous moon, and I was flowing out to meet him.

This was not the first time my heart had to stretch beyond my mind to understand and allow this love. And it would not be the last.

But the sturdy root of trust sustained my passage.

The shimmering stars became my silent chanting.

And at 1:30 in the morning, we were awakened by a shout, and saw two headlamps bobbing down the road. Two thirsty, hungry climbers had returned, muscles steaming and eyes on fire with the single-pointed focus that had powered them up the massive gray rock all day. They spoke of a "gruesome" seven-hour descent, accompanied by the rising moon. Their minds and bodies had become the mountain.

My partner and I embraced, filled with gratitude. Early in our relationship, we'd promised each other our love would be a source of freedom. Oh, how that's been tested over the years! But standing there in the raw joy of our meeting, each of our breaths renewed this vow.

Was this embrace a prayer? Was it prayer as the silent rope coiled and uncoiled all day long, as they held each others' lives in their hands? Was it prayer when they quenched their thirst with drops of water from the moss growing in the crevices of the cliff after getting off route?

I ask these questions, because I haven't been sure how to speak about "Zen prayer." It would seem we don't pray, since we don't orient ourselves toward an external authority. And for what would I pray, since our practice is to be present with each moment just as it is?

I am helped by the words of the late Zen teacher Dainin Katagiri, who spoke about the "interacting communion of appeal and response." He wrote, "There is nothing to ask for help from in this world, but there is something we can appeal to beyond the human world, even if we don't know exactly what it is. To do that we pray for our lives, for others' lives, to the vastness of space and existence. . . . Then, the response comes from the whole universe. We appeal for help, and simultaneously, the universe reaches out its hand" (from *Returning to Silence*, 82–83).

Sometimes the opening to the universe appears to be outside — when I make my appeal to the sky, to Great Nature. Other times, I find my place in the universe by sitting still and going inside. I do this in zazen, the fundamental practice of Zen Buddhism. I sit in silence on the meditation cushion, settling into my body and breath, relaxing my mind into awareness of the present moment.

Katagiri equates zazen with prayer. He writes about zazen as the practice of manifesting the source of our life. "Buddhism is not a revealed religion, but an awakened religion — awakening to the self, or to the truth" (98).

How to do this is as individual as are the different paths of our lives. When I first began practicing zazen, I was discouraged. I thought "good zazen" meant my mind would always be calm. Sometimes it is. Sometimes zazen is a deep relief, to finally pause in my busy-ness and feel the slow rhythm of my lungs, or enjoy the sounds and smells of the day. But often my mind is restless, or obsessive. So for me, "awakening to the self, to the truth" has meant learning to be willing and able to taste myself as I am. The posture and stillness of zazen has offered a container: a safe place to explore what arises, keep things cooking, and discover what this alchemical process might reveal.

Here is a personal example of sitting through a time of difficulty, sitting with my self-concerned "small mind" and slowly, through zazen, letting it open up to "big mind" — Buddha's mind — the spacious awareness that holds everything.

Many years ago, I was in a group of people who went through a challenging period of change. One of the people in the group responded to the circumstances with tremendous anger, and what I felt was overly rigid and hurtful behavior. Hour after hour during zazen, I seethed with rage about this person. I generated fantasies about the terrible things I wished would happen to teach him a lesson.

But after several weeks of this, I grew sick of my hateful thoughts. Even though I still thought I was *right*, nonetheless I realized I needed to intervene in this obsession. I needed to study my anger, rather than perpetuate myself as its victim. I needed to — as contemporary Zen scholar Taigen Dan Leighton said once in a lecture — "become intimate with the way the affliction of ignorance operates in our hearts and minds. Study our own delusion, our own suffering."

So I shifted the focus of my attention from spinning the story of why this person was so bad and I was so righteous to just sitting with my pounding heart. Letting myself experience the tightness in my chest. My clenched jaw. My shallow breath. I became aware of a deep ache beneath my physical tightness. A feeling of sadness.

I appealed to the universe for help. This time, the response was the Buddhist practice of *metta* — the intentional wishing of goodwill to self and others. *May I release my judgment. May he be free from hatred. May my heart be open to the world.*

A thought came to me: *People don't usually hurt others unless they've been hurt themselves.* As I sensed the suffering that could lead to such a rigid defense, my heart began to soften for this person. And then I began to touch my own suffering. There were actually aspects of our mutual circumstance that were difficult for me, too. I was scared. In fact, I was angry! How much easier it was to be mad at *him* for *his* anger, rather than have to face my own.

The hard edges defining "me" and "him" began to dissolve. I wrote in my journal, "Anger is part of the web. Anger is the voice of pain and suffering, unconsciously passed on through the generations. Today I feel calm. Who knows what will happen?"

I have since found that this experience — of feeling self and other dissolve into the same interconnecting web; of softening the heart, relaxing the talons of the mind, loosening the strands of the self-reinforcing story — is one which reliably occurs if I just sit long enough. Even if I still don't always "like" zazen, it has become the foundational practice which supports my life.

And I couldn't do it alone. I am so grateful for my teacher, Sobun Katherine Thanas, and the community of people (*sangha*) with whom I practice. Through shared daily ritual, through the volunteer labor which runs the temple, we create a place to sit together, offer encouragement to one another, and evolve a life-long conversation about how to bring the mindful attention of our zazen out into the world.

Every morning after zazen, we have service — our daily communal prayer. To the deep resonance of the bronze bell, we press our hands together in *gassho*, a few inches from our heart. Nine times, we bow, dropping to the floor. Homage to big mind. Homage to Buddha. To the awakened being, whose potential dwells within each human heart and mind. We chant together, honoring our ancestors, renewing our vows. After service, we do a brief period of silent temple cleaning. Dusting off the meditation cushions. Sweeping the floor. Refreshing the flowers. Then we gather in a circle and exchange a few words before going off to our jobs and families.

So I have discovered that my "interacting communion of appeal and response" is threefold: with the great vast universe, with my own inner wisdom and compassion, and with all my relations — my sangha, friends, family, clients, neighbors — and all those who challenge me as well.

I pray I can keep growing stronger in fully meeting and engaging with the world — bringing forth my Buddha nature, and receiving the Buddha nature of all sentient beings.

Prayer in a Dark Time

Brian Gleason

*One man's prayerful vision of a helping hand
across the cold, raging waters of addiction...*

I WAS INTRODUCED to crystal meth, or speed, at a bar in
San Francisco. Like many others before me and many
to follow, I was passed a line, I hesitated, and then without
a lot more thinking I snorted it back into my brain. And the
party was off. And what a party it was, but that is no longer
the story to tell, if it ever really was. The story to tell is of
a man looking desperately for something, a man praying in
his own way.

◆ ◆ ◆

There's a ritual quality to it. I spill the bag of crystals onto
a mirror I have laid across the table because that's the way
I saw someone else do it. Now I do it, because I want to see
where it takes me. I like to travel. Destination unknown —
some time ago, never mind how long, I began realizing that
the journey may be the only thing.

I use a credit card to crunch the crystals into a powder. The guy I'd watched before used a razor blade but I

freak on sharp objects and damn near faint at the sight of
blood — a queasy traveler, the kind that takes Dramamine
before going out on a boat. Crunch crunch crunch p-ching!
One of the crystals shoots across the mirror rather than
submit to Visa. I flock it back in with the rest and start
crunching perpendicular to my last pattern, the whole routine being methodical, lablike — a kind of spellcast quality
to it; trancelike; Zen. I'd experienced that in a part-time
job once. As a dishwasher you have a task — it's a simple
task — you do the task and then you move on to the next
task. Dirty dish. Rinse and soap dish. Clean dish. Next dish.
The complications of work and love and life in general since
that job had not brought with them a concomitant measure
of happiness. But I wasn't doing this for happiness.

I stare at my little white beach, pausing for a moment.
With my driver's license (an equally harmless tool), I scrape
the residue from the credit card into the pile, then the credit
card on the driver's license, back and forth until only a trace
holds out on the edges of both. This trace I wipe on my pant
leg and brush to the floor where it mingles unnoticed with
the dust. Pause. This is just recreation, I say. I am only going
to do this once.

I arrange the pile into lines that turn out roughly equal in
size for no other reason than the overall methodical nature
of things to this point. Almost ready. I roll up a dollar bill
for the next part, the preferred method of a sawed-off straw
conjuring another assortment of ugly images — I have to

distance myself somehow. My hands start to shake. I lose the tautness in the dollar bill and have to refold it. A few breaths and I am ready. I shove the chair back, crane my neck in, take a breath, tip the bill at the base of a line and take it in. I know it's going to hurt so I lean back, breathing through my mouth. A few moments — then the burn! A jet of ice through the back of my head and down my neck. I pound my fist into my thigh but feel nothing except the fire in my brain. Then it's gone. I breathe through my nose, pinching off a sniff almost in defiance. It flushes through to the back of my throat. I swallow, and enjoy the awful, toxic taste.

My hands shake — in anticipation this time. Already a craving? Maybe I'm hooked. The dollar bill still curled tight, I set it at the tip of the next line, taking it in without pause. Sweet burn! Sniff back — and the taste. I hardly notice the taste this time. Maybe I notice and start to like it. Strange craving. One more line is enough. I credit-card the rest into the little drug bag, tucking it in the change pocket of my jeans.

Seconds. The physical rush surrounds and embraces in warmth and tingles and redness as I get up out of my chair. A bead of sweat breaks loose, slow-crawling down my forehead. I smile. I throw on some ambient music and sit against the bed, on the floor, staring up, the rush coursing through, igniting my skin to a red tingle. I wipe my forehead. I pinch a sniff back and swallow, tasting it all the way through to my stomach.

Somewhere along the street on my way down to the bars the feeling hits me. The fire dance. Tears and madness. I go to my favorite bars where I like the music and the bodies and the dark and the sex. I want to be as close as possible to *it*. Everything before this moment is a monastery. I'm hungry, and what I don't realize is that it is already too late. The music dies and the clubs close and I wander the streets now, mocking the cool fogged air with my warmth. But even that is starting to go, and I get cold. There's a fall coming, a dropping off into something dark and deep, a drop cushioned by memory, which is little more than a tingle through my skin, last vestiges of the drug rescuing me for a moment; a receding moment. I snatch back, but snatching is the hunger so it's already too late.

It's very cold now. The hunger pulls at me, stabbing.

After all the drugs, all the advice, all the counseling and research and self-searching, it was finally an image from a dream that caught me. Whether it was in answer to a prayer or something sent on its own I still do not know. I only know that it caught and held me, and led me places I could never have found on my own. In this brief but lasting image, a man standing on one side of a raging river reaches his hand out for me to cross, and I stand trembling on the other side, shaking in every bone. When I reach across I feel love and loss equally, and can hardly hang on.

The image stayed with me like a near miss, a stray bullet past my head whispering, "Look around, or what you do not see may hit you." I told this dream — this image — to a friend, and something in me prodded to follow with my whole story of life from the past several years — my drug story, my story of a search, my prayer. My friend listened. I slept on his couch that night. The next day he took me to a recovery meeting, starting me on a journey that has now lasted several years. In hundreds of recovery meetings, I sat and listened and talked with others who had also tenuously held out their hand to meet the person on the other side of the raging river, the one who would pull them across.

In recovery, in my work with others in a similar struggle and their work with me, in the quiet moments that now came to me, I felt the presence of the other, reaching across the river. It was not so important whether I made it across the water or not, and eventually I was going to fall in any-way — what became of vital, lasting importance was the *feeling* of reaching across.

This feeling became my prayer. Recovery meetings, watching for images in dreams and in life, working with others — all of this became my ritual. Carefully and methodically, not unlike the way that I once chopped crystal meth shards into powder, I watch for fragile images, I listen for soft voices; I go back to that least explored place — small flame in a dark wind, fire trying to breathe. I saw something in an image,

I heard something in a meeting, I felt something in an embrace, and now I long for it. It's like a glance from a stranger I always knew and never met, a story told by someone lying beside me while I slept, a poem I'm trying to remember, a prayer I want to say. It is a prayer to you, a shout back that I hear your whisper.

We live in what Joseph Campbell described as a time between myths. We stand naked before a God we are not even sure is listening, and we fear not so much his wrath as his indifference. We stand on the other side of the river, trembling from being left alone so long, reaching across in blackness and a strange kind of courage that comes from just not knowing any more. Maybe it was just this awareness that I sought through my years of drug use and excessive living. Maybe I had to shatter the illusion in my own way, face my nakedness, dance and weep in it, then, tired and lonely, reach across and wait for a hand. I do not know what was on the other side, but something held me, and I am grateful, for the water below is deep and cold.

Prayer a la cucina

Lauri D. Goldenhersh

*A favorite prayer from the kitchen . . .
good, hearty, earthy soup.*

START WITH OLIVE OIL, a slippery and aromatic result of long sunny days and careful harvesting. Sauté onions and garlic until golden, then add plenty of water or a good stock base. The fluid itself is the life force of soup, activated by fire to mingle flavors and swirling energy.

My favorite prayer *a la cucina* is soup. It is an inventive and always unique melding of the four elements which feels like creation, led by the divine, and lends me peace and connection to an ancient process that is somehow beyond us and therefore magical.

So, we have water, and fire, of course. (Cold soup is against my gastronomical religion.) Earth comes in vegetables, beans, and if you wish, meat. Root vegetables like potatoes, onions, beets, and carrots feel more earthy than others, fresh from such a recent immersion in the soil itself. Their hearty textures add body to the soup, making a luxurious bed for their crisper counterparts to lie in. Other vegetables taste of sun and crisp air: broccoli, tomatoes, asparagus, sweet red and yellow peppers. Mushrooms, corn, and beans lend rich flavor. Garlic blends and wafts, working in two directions at once. This aromatic communion with the ether is like an olfactory smoke signal to the universe: "I'm here, and we're in this together."

I am not a culinary high priestess. I do not have a cooking show or my own catch phrase. I'm just a home cook who has found many levels of satisfaction in food: physical, emotional, intellectual, and yes, spiritual. Creating a new recipe is one way I connect with the earth and with God. Cooking and working with ingredients becomes an ongoing prayer of thanks, a sacrament in and of itself, at least mildly ritualized from the selection of vegetables to the celebration of the final bite. I don't necessarily consume more than my share of cookbooks or food shows, but am deeply drawn to movies and books that express a similar connection: *Babette's Feast*, *Tortilla Soup*, the definitive *Like Water for Chocolate*, and Chitra Banerjee Divakaruni's excellent *The Mistress of Spices* are all evocative examples of how food symbolizes life and love and the search for meaning.

Some days, selecting and prepping vegetables may be the closest I get to a nature excursion, because in the urban/suburban commute of Los Angeles, much of my time tends to move from building to road, building to road. Finding a beautiful bouquet of broccolini, large and leafy oyster mushrooms, or an exquisite batch of miniature cippolini onions serves up inspiration for a sojourn into the infinite variety of creation, and I can't wait to get home to get started. With each slice of the knife, aromas enter my soul and become a prayer of thanks. Small bits of scallion, cilantro, or lemongrass offer up scents so distinctive that they spark memories of travels years ago. Onions and sweet peppers are sliced carefully into long strips, working with the grain. Large chunks of carrot, potato, and fresh squash offer something to chew on. Chopping and culling the best bits from my plunder, I have to chuckle at my always-eager black pug, parked under the pull-out cutting board, ears perked and sitting at tiptoed attention, anticipating the wayward fall of anything colorful. (He's not so fond of broccoli; tomatoes are his favorite.)

Art and magic lie in the seasonings: salt and pepper are standard, and herbs like thyme, dill, parsley, tarragon, mustard, and celery seeds can be a good start. But my eclectic cupboard also offers tastes to suit the mix of the day: the flavors of fenugreek or Mexican epazote wrap gently around everything they touch. Lemon juice or vinegar lightens and balances dark flavors, and habañero or Thai chiles, added tiny bit by bit, add just the right amount of bite, even for a wimp like me. Add roasted sesame oil, black mustard seeds, my favorite Guyanese curry powder, or even a touch of Vietnamese cinnamon, and the tightrope dance of highs and lows is done, ready to simmer to a marvelous conclusion.

The heat from the stove ignites spices from within, spreading each grain through the pot, across the room, and up through my neighbor's balcony. The complex and layered aroma is a grand composition, my symphony, my song of praise. Having brought together water and fire, earth and sky, all I can do is complete the ritual by ladling soup into a bowl, warming my face in the rising haze, and finding a warm chair where I can be grateful with every bite.

I Feel Prayer
Is Much Abused

NORMAN MAILER

*A literary and cultural icon
talks about prayer.*

LET ME SAY that I haven't prayed to God since I was a
child. I believe God exists. I believe He is Good and
that He is Powerful. But not all Good and not all Powerful.
He's opposed by Satan. I believe that too. I believe that particular war lies at the core of all of our human psychology
as well. I don't pray because the central metaphor I have
for God is that he is a worthy, heroic, and tired general,
and the last thing he needs is a few more complaints from
his troops, which, of course, is what I believe we are. Some
of us are better than others; some of us try to be honor-
able; some of us are aware of our capacity for treachery. An
army in short. I feel prayer is much abused. I can see the
belief and the goodness and the solace that people receive
from it, so I would not stand in judgment of the prayers of
others. But I loathe the species of prayer that indulges in

nothing but emoluments to God. How bored God must be with all that praise if He is anything near like all Good and all Powerful. It's the weak who need praise. My distrust of prayer is founded on that. It is an arrogance of the worst sort in my religious opinion to believe that God needs our praise. The only exception I might make for this is when a parent prays to God for the life of their child, when a boy or a girl is very ill.

Presence of the Holy

J. Jon Bruno

*Through prayer, a law enforcement officer who kills a man
in the line of duty eventually finds wholeness and another way
in which to serve . . . as a bishop of the church.*

YEARS AGO when I was a law enforcement officer, I killed a man in the line of duty. I was unable to find solitude or comfort afterward. Even though society said I had done a needed thing and I received an award for good conduct and bravery, the very center of my being was disquieted. Anger, frustration, and confusion became watchwords of my life.

Earlier in my life I'd searched for a future of service, wanting to become the person God intended me to be. This seemed to mean becoming an active force in the world. Yet, as a boy, my life was based on a victory orientation. I had a desire to win in athletics in order to prove my worth. When my father tried to teach me about reflection, I didn't understand him. Wouldn't perfection of action bring me the ability to achieve my goals? I wanted to become a professional athlete and was well on my way. Life intervened, however, when a bodily injury wiped out all such possibilities. Slowly I came to realize my father's advice saying that reflection was to be an important tool. But how? Where did I want to go?

Somewhere in the back of my mind was the idea of becoming an Episcopal priest, yet I wasn't willing or able to accept this as reality. I looked for another helping profession. This is how I turned into a law enforcement officer. Now, after the incident when I killed a man in the line of duty, I gradually found solace in my worship and faith tradition. Then, at the urging of my priest and bishop, I moved forward with the idea of enrolling in a seminary.

But even after doing so, a disquieting pain remained at the center of my being. What could I do about it? Gradually I learned how to meditate in the presence of the holy. The way of prayer led me toward a life's journey toward wholeness. A major part of this was relinquishing a search for perfection. Instead, I learned that I required openness, surrender, and centeredness.

Paul Tillich, the theologian, identified the ultimate concern of our life as being the focus of our prayer. Every day I look for that day's ultimate concern. It becomes the focus of my meditation for the day. This might be the sickness or death of someone. Or a serious social matter. Or a pressing need for reconciliation. I try to focus on this, allowing it room in my mind. I come to a point of clarity about what I need to do.

There are some guidelines in my spiritual practice. Usually I get up at 5:30 a.m. and sit in silence in order to clear my mind. I start to focus on the name Jesus. This opens my heart and mind to the presence of the holy. Midday, I return to a meditative state. Has God altered my day? Are there other opportunities for service? Now I feel ready for the rest of the day, refreshed and nourished, focused on how God calls me to be in community.

I realize that my earlier search for perfection led me to block the presence of Jesus. Now I've learned that Jesus speaks to me at the center of my being when I am willing to listen in the presence of the holy.

God, Keep Me in the Music

David Avshalomov

*Through writing music, a composer slowly wakes up
to a prayerful spirituality. . . .*

I WAS RAISED without prayer. Our household had no
religion. My father is a nonobserving secular Jew, a
composer and conductor who had, at most, set a few Old
Testament liturgical texts to music when young. My mother,
of Scandinavian heritage and raised Lutheran, became a
sort of mildly pagan-style pantheist (though later in life she
returned to church periodically after her mom died). She
loves nature and celebrates it in poetry.

Growing up, I knew about churches and worship and
liturgical music — my mom took me to church a few times,
and I loved the group singing of hymns. My high school
choir sang some Palestrina and Mozart, my dad was a classical musician, and I heard plenty of Western Classical church
music and studied it in college — but just as music. Then
at Harvard I sang in the Memorial Church choir (as a paid

job) and sat through endless sermons and droning responsive readings and stilted improvised prayers, unaffected —
waiting for the spiritual joy I felt in singing the next anthem
or hymn (even though I did not "believe" in the religious
message of the texts). You can see where this was leading.
Gradually music took on a larger role in my slow spiritual
awakening. Eventually I realized *consciously* that I felt the
divine through music, particularly song.

After my wife Randi and I started practicing Judaism
as adults and joined a temple for our children's benefit, I
was urged to sing bass in their faltering choir for the High
Holy Days, and soon was asked to revitalize it. The next
year I doubled its size and hired a professional conductor, and our amazing cantor, a true *shileach tzibur* (emissary
of the congregation), whose singing really made us feel he
was expressing our group feelings directly to God, commis-
sioned me to write a new setting of the *kedushah* for him
and them — the prayer "holy, holy, holy, Lord God of all,
Heaven and Earth are full of Your Glory." As a grown boy
who'd never had a *bar mitzvah* and was still learning to do
the prayers right at services, I was stunned and humbled
and joyful.

I took this as a sacred trust. For me, the writing of music
to set a prayer required assuming a prayerful attitude, along
with my best professional skills and a hope for inspiration.
(The composer Franz Josef Haydn is said to have knelt each
morning and prayed to God for just one usable musical

theme, and he always came up with one. I've also seen manuscript replicas of his scores where he inscribed the last page "*fine. laus Deo*" [the end. Praise God]. I knew how he felt.) The cantor broke the text down for me, to the individual syllable, and I worked very hard to make a worthy piece for performance before the augmented congregation that shows up every year. He and the choir sang it beautifully, with true feeling, and it was a success — even the rabbi got a little teary. I have done further settings since, and my approach is always the same.

But as for prayer *per se*, I still don't really consider myself a particularly prayerful person, nor a deeply spiritual one. I'm still just waking up. I never learned the regular practice of standardized prayer as a normal, induced habit. I'm not an Orthodox man in ritual garments doing the full sets several times across the day. That's heavy duty, and I don't think I could go there. Instead, I've come to religious practice and group prayer by individual choice and as something to learn slowly, in a context offering a lot of options about how and when I pray, and why. It's more like remedial education. I'm still deciding what I really believe about it. Some ritualized prayers speak for me, others not; and sometimes I can enter into improvised solo prayer in a sincere way.

There is one more dimension of my approach to prayer. Outside of and even prior to my Jewish awakening, there was my odd practice of occasional prayer in and about nature. Long before I reclaimed my preferred hereditary religion, and parallel to my awakening to music of the soul, I also began to develop an expanding awareness of the sacredness of nature (which is a candle I think my mom lit for me, though not explicitly). In particular, for example, I consider old-growth forests sacred places, and I plant trees in mountains as an exercise of contrition and remediation. Over the last thirty years, during my search and struggle for a vital role as a master musician in society, I developed an increasing yearning to be in nature, in wilderness, to be where everything around me felt *right* and where I felt at home, more than in urban society.

I remember that the very first time I felt a spontaneous impulse to sing the *Sh'ma* (the first prayer of Jews, "Hear, Israel: the Lord our God, the Lord is one") out loud was as I scrambled up once onto the gently sloping back end of Lembert Dome by Tuolumne Meadows in Yosemite National Park (a sacred place if ever there was one). I let loose, and it felt great, a way to express joy and wonder and gratitude. Imagine my surprise and secret pleasure to learn later that the Talmud also teaches that we are closer to God in mountains and wilderness. For me, mountain and forest walking had always been a kind of meditation on wonder, if not actual prayer. And over the years, as I have sought long walks there, I have repeatedly found that there comes a moment in each trek, combining somehow the arrival at an awesome place, perhaps a grand or special view, and a state of deep exertion and elevated metabolism, that bubbles up in a moment of humble gratitude (often near sunset), and I think or say out loud my private mountain version of the *shehecheyanu* (a traditional prayer that thanks Adonai for preserving us to see a particular moment): "Thank you, big guy, for letting me come out here, be up here, in this glory, yet another time."

Away from wilderness, music is my way of seeing and entering the world of humans, but it is also my way of connecting to my deepest, nonconceptual, nonverbal, non-abstract self — and from there to the divine and to the divine in others, if I can. And if that is what prayer does, then perhaps that is my best or most personal prayer, though I rarely say it: "God, keep me in the music, and let me connect to others with my music, and may my work be acceptable in your hearing and in theirs, for God help me, I can't stop it, it's what I do; you gave me the gift, I am grateful and almost helpless before its power when I feel it in me, so please keep me on the right path in using it."

O Thou! O Thou!

FREDERICK BUECHNER

*A much-loved American writer
describes his prayer life.*

A GREAT DEAL of my ragged and sporadic praying has to do with the physical safety of my children and grandchildren. I pray that their plane be surrounded by light, that the captain and crew know what they're doing, that they encounter no danger either from within or from without. Rabbit's foot prayers. Knocking on wood prayers. When some horror like the tsunami happens, the suffering is so vast that I can't imagine even God's being able to do anything about it and pray only that he be somewhere present in the unholy mess of it to bring healing and peace out of it. I pray for people I know who are sick or in trouble when I happen to think of them. Sometimes I try to picture Jesus coming to them and laying his hands upon their heads. Sometimes I pray for the beloved dead. I pray often when I am driving the car. Sometimes a great flood of thanksgiving wells up in me at some moment so beautiful and holy, some day so gorgeous, some unexpected turn of events so joyous, that all I can do is say O Thou! O Thou!

The prayer that brings me greatest peace and comfort is the Twenty-third Psalm. I have no set times or places for prayer, no list of people to pray for. Maybe whole days will go by when I hardly pray at all. But I have a dim sense that somewhere, deep inside, some version of who I am is always at it. Is God listening, whatever that means? I hope so, pray so. More often than not I believe so. More often than not I feel that there is a listener.

Prayer in City Hall

Marc B. Haefele

A hardened reporter's prayers of intercession.

ROBERTA DOESN'T GET to see daylight in her work. She is pale with a subterranean pallor. Close to retirement age, her hair still describably blond, tied back in a severe bun or scraggly ponytail, her work habitat is one of the deepest of City Hall's subsurface parking garages. But she says, "Have a blessed day" to anyone she encounters. It's a spirit she has — one that fifteen years ago pushed her to surround her workplace with glowing holiday memorabilia — electric Christmas Santas, inner-lit Halloween pumpkins, white shining Easter doves on strings, dozens of them, circling the old walnut desk she used back then, a desk that had probably belonged to some forgotten middling official upstairs, way back in Eisenhower's time.

Then this spirit so filled her that she sought and got more AIDS Walk pledges than any other parking lot employee. She was possessed by that spirit of hers. It took her into the offices of top officials, even elected ones. Of course, she first waylaid those of us who used her garage. Then, in lunch and break times, she went far upstairs to the sunlit realms, and strode past receptionists, past security guards, blundering into sancta and vital meetings with her little smile and high faded voice, asking for money to save lives, to help her splendid cause. The cause was helped, surely, but not her career, because her zeal got her fatally noticed by some very powerful people. Who was, they asked one another, this little person in the scruffy, mismatched uniform and granny glasses who kept pushing into places she had no right to be, demanding pledges? In the end she got her big award for fund raising, but was further recognized by reassignment to an above-ground parking lot, exposed to the torrid downtown sun and infrequent rain and cold, most of a mile's walk from City Hall. There she repined for years before being allowed back to a closer one, deep in the friendly earth. Where, if you happen to run into her as you walk to your car, she still offers you a blessed day and asks that the Lord keep you happy and well.

That's where a little too much religiosity can get you with the bureaucracy. City government is obviously not a theocracy, and it's usually cool to any sustained zealotry that isn't secular. But it's been my habitat, my work environment, now, for nearly twenty-seven years. I've learned to treasure the little godly things one does see there — like Roberta's feckless, successful, and indifferently rewarded blessedness. Heaven knows there are not enough people like her. There are good people in city government, and bad. And mostly

there are those who can be both, so you always have to notice the invisible and often all too visible signs. Sometimes
you can figure it. Sometimes you can't. And sometimes, you
have to relegate the decision to a Higher Power. And make
sure to keep your own very strong feelings out of it — you
have such feelings of course, everyone knows you do, although you aren't supposed to have them, being a member
of the press, of the Fourth Estate. Whose purpose, as one
inspired clergyman once put it, is to bring more truth into
the world.

For the most part, that our governments are secular is a
terribly good thing. Just look at the history of the periods
when our clergy had the power of the law, not to mention
life or death, over citizens. In one's own life, however, sep-
aration of church and state is another matter. One terrific
thing about a journalistic career is that it breaks open the
casements of oneself. You can't hide from much. Even the
divine. In my career as a reporter, God and His manifestations played small parts from the beginning. There was
the traditional Methodist New Year's ceremony I covered
in New Jersey in 1980 that brought back to me the very
idea of worship and congregation. A couple years later,
there was the murder trial in Santa Ana, when the witness braced herself to give crucial testimony against the
giggling psychopath who'd killed her best friend: "God give
me strength!" This was a powerful exclamation — but it was

more: it was a prayer. And in this case, it was a prayer that was answered.

Maybe that it was answered for this poor, sobbing soul by a just criminal conviction was one of the many things that edged me out of my convinced secularism: The witness reached for strength and it was given her. I was then new to California, a big strange world in which it seemed I couldn't make a move without making a mistake. I had no friends, I had no money. My strength, it seemed unavailing. I did not know my way around in every literal and figurative sense, though in three years, I lived in dozens of places, none of them permanent, all over this vast four-thousand-square-mile map. I was conscious of the fact that in my transience, in my lack of any social anchor or personal sense of place, I was not a great deal different from many of the sad people whose solitary violent or accidental deaths I reported in places like Burbank and Compton. I remember I feared this fate for everyone I saw who was, like me, at loose ends and fearful in Southern California. Where too often, you came for the ecstasy, and stayed for the dread. When I was young I prayed too much. We prayed a lot in our family, sort of like we ate and slept, but for what I can't recall, since we never really lacked for anything important in our lower–upper-middle-class existence; except, perhaps, family happiness. My mother and father prayed for divine guidance every step of their lives. They affirmed that they always got such guidance, but if they did, it did neither of them any good that I saw. Bad decisions got made anyway. Our family gradually fell apart: I was sent away to school as a problem child, my mother became a perpetual invalid, my father a rage-filled, frustrated man. We left, finally, with what I was assured had been the utmost prayerful deliberation, our gorgeous country home for a smelly, faraway city where my father's new career rapidly crashed. The parents kept on praying, but my mother kept on suffering and my father kept on raging and screaming at us until he was out of a job and she died. I was off on my own by then, my own marriage sliding away, but I came to stay with my father then and listened to him. His rage was gone for a time, and I liked to hear him ask questions about death, child-like questions like, where do we go when we die, questions he'd never asked before. All that prayer, I thought, and no useful answers to a simple basic thing like that. I had been reading poets for answers to such questions for some time. I was by then what you could certainly call prayer-averse. A few months later, though, I found myself working in this city and becoming religious myself. I was doing police reporting on one of the nation's highest murder rates. It is an honest apprehension when you enter into this serious side of journalism to wonder whether you will be changed by what you see and write about. Socially, this probability is made light of: we reporters tell ourselves that firefighters, cops, and paramedics really handle the grim stuff, we just describe it, write it down. You have to change, though.

Most people can't do the job right otherwise. You can't be shocked anymore, and any emotional reactions you have must stay out of your work. That doesn't mean they can't show up elsewhere in your life. That is a common hazard.

One easy solution is to start to think like a cop. To desensitize. To joke about the many "misdemeanor murders" among poor people. To maintain that in the barrios, gunshot wounds are a natural cause of death. This sort of thing doesn't help you much. I doubt it really helps the cops. But it is a companionable attitude. It is a way to talk to one another about something that is, innately, pretty hard to talk about. Particularly after Saturday night, when you finished up at 7:00 a.m. the next morning, writing down the last details of the deaths by violence of the previous dozen hours or so, from your desk in the back of the police station, where the whole world moaned at you over radios and telephones. What to do with the morning after such a night's work became something of a puzzle to me. No matter how bright shone the sun, the world looked terribly bleak. Breakfast, then bedtime are an odd combination. I lived in a beautiful place then, where the ocean crashed on the shore a few yards from my front porch. Some mornings, I could sit and look out at the Pacific, its birds, its dolphins, for hours without feeling any better.

If I had been a Christian then, I would have lost my religion. Instead, I found it. It came slowly, to be sure. There was the example of a certain wild and devout young reporter

I'd known early in my career. How could she be both those things and such a good person too? Others I met in my work who similarly based their lives and were the better for it. I had gone for so many years without being close to a religious person who did not in some way seem to me like a credulous fool. So one Sunday morning, instead of finding myself on the porch at 8:00 a.m. thinking dwindling thoughts of mayhem over a cooling cup of coffee, why did I find myself sitting in church? Of course, you could wonder what any of us congregants were doing, so shortly after dawn on a Sunday morning, mumbling our psalms in unison, kneeling to confess our sins, most of us, perhaps, seeking shelter of some kind from the events of the night so recently passed.

It was the prayers of the intercession that taught me to pray — for others.

We may have, must have, prayed for other people outside our family when I was young. But I don't remember doing so. Now I'd pray for the perfect strangers I encountered at several removes in my work, of course. For someone I'd never met nor would I meet, but had written about the previous midnight, who was still clinging to life in a North Valley ICU. This prayer thing was also a great way not to think too much of oneself, verily, to annihilate self-pity, which I then carried around in abundance. To pray for others, struggling for life or dead by violence, was to be grateful that one was simply alive, earning fifty dollars a day; a prayer for others was a prayer of gratitude for one's own life: one had almost no money but, for a year or two, a good place to live in. A healthy body and a few good friends. No outstanding warrants. No bullet wounds. No dead children.

When I was finally promoted to the above-ground, daylight realms of City Hall, I felt exalted. Keeping normal hours, wearing normal working clothes, eating normal lunches at normal lunch hour. Every little bit of daily tactilia that I had taken for granted a couple of career steps before and thought I had lost forever came back renewed and blessed. I had a fine sixty-year-old office, normal people to talk to every hour of the day, and stories to write about lawmaking and events that never ended in tragedy. God had chosen to put me back among the living. This was good, but it was from those dark nights of work with the maimed and dying that I learned to pray again — though very rarely, and mostly for others. Prayer is such a precious thing, I don't want to impose. And there are so many people who need God's help more than I do.

Laughing with God

FELIX RACELIS

A playwright offers up humor as a prayerful activity.

ONE OF THE BIG QUESTIONS is why God would ever allow such uneven and mediocre movie representations throughout the years. Okay, the burning bush in *The Ten Commandments* was pretty good. (Although I've seen Christmas trees that were more spectacular.) But even when you add up all the disembodied voices, Charlton Heston still had way more lines.

I'm grateful that in the intervening years God switched agents, because finally there's one good film depiction. I'm referring to *Dogma*, where God was a diminutive, anorexic-looking female hippie who enjoyed disappearing from the heavenly court to run off to arcades and play skeeball. At last, a film portrayal of God with a sense of humor. I understood and appreciated.

Let me explain.

About ten years ago I was asked by the rector of the church where I worshiped to give a stewardship pitch to our congregation. Standing before large crowds of people and delivering speeches is never a favorite activity. It is somewhere down there with tooth extraction and traffic school.

But at a point I wanted to insert a bit of humor. Some folks laughed and eased the way. My fraying nerves suddenly felt comfortable and assured, and I had the wherewithal to land a couple of one-liners and even ad lib. As I rattled off reasons for supporting the church, my mind filled with a new thought: "God has a warped sense of humor."

As I grow in my prayer life, I find God has an odd ability to push me forward in ways I could never have imagined. Only a few years ago I had sat in those same pews and witnessed another parishioner give just such a stewardship speech. Then I reassured myself I would never be caught doing that. However, now here I was — one of the least likely suspects — actually enjoying what I had regarded as a unique form of public humiliation and torture. In that moment, I understood God had a truly weird sense of humor I could appreciate too.

Is That Your Final Answer?

I often imagine the joke's on me, particularly when I have this recurring vision/dream. I'm approaching heaven's gates (why do they look strangely like those at Paramount Studios in Hollywood?). St. Peter is about to open up, but first he's got a few questions. And no, I can't call a friend.

I think I've got the answers. He doesn't care whether I did yard sales for the church, or tithed, or sat on a committee outreaching multicultural youth and senior urban/suburban socioeconomic geodemographic clusters. He doesn't even care that I served time in a parish leadership capacity. But he has three questions: Did I forgive others and myself? Did I learn humility? Did I love my brother/sister? And then I wake up.

All in the Timing

Most comedians agree that their success depends on timing. It took me a while to understand that — to realize God's timing and timeline are different from mine. When I pray I often give God a laundry list of things I want Her to do, along with preferred deadlines. When I began playwriting I wanted to be a produced playwright. Yet God had different plans. I experienced several years of writing and rejection as a beginning playwright. But some time later, when I'd become better prepared and a better writer, I finally did get produced.

As a young man, I had a rocky relationship with my father. I left home as quickly as I could, chose a profession my father not only didn't understand but couldn't pronounce, and tried to be as different from him as possible. Later I discovered my father did the very same things, too. He had moved even farther away from home than I did. And now relatives tell me I resemble my father more than ever! Yikes! I don't think God's punch lines are any less funny, even if they arrive decades later.

Divine Comedian

As I mature, I'm convinced that God is a comedic genius. You can never be sure when She's about to bound onto your stage, like an over-the-top character in a Feydeau farce. Or barging in through a doorway sporting a gigantic handlebar moustache, and wielding a peacock feather to tickle you. Or maybe even challenge you to a game of skeeball.

Can a Film Be a Prayer?

Stephen Vittoria

A filmmaker says, "Absolutely."

I BELIEVE that all forms of private and/or public communication can be a prayer if the person or group crafting the prayer desires change...change that corrects injustice, that sets people free, that heals hate with love, fear with compassion, change that wipes out ignorance with understanding, and then ultimately, change that saves lives — both spiritual and physical. And a film, be it thirty seconds or two hours, can be a significant agent of change given that unselfish prayer is a revolutionary act usually demanding change, and in most cases the transformation sought through prayer requires tectonic shifts in behavior. Rarely does prayer seek to perpetuate the status quo.

Throughout the history of cinema one can cite abundant examples of celluloid stories (now video) that coexisted as prayers — petitions for change in the hearts and minds of those audiences sitting passively in the dark. To witness film as prayer, the skeptic in us only needs to screen F. W. Murnau's 1927 masterpiece *Sunrise*, the German director's seminal work about corruption and redemption. This love story, subtitled *A Song of Two Humans*, is an archetype for film as prayer — the classic awakening of conscience in the human soul as the husband chooses peace over violence, good over evil, redemption over sin. In this case and in countless others, filmmaking can be defined as an act of fellowship and prayer aimed at suggesting change through a deeper understanding of the people we live with and the world we inhabit.

Now, do all films qualify as a prayer? Of course not — so how do we decide what qualifies and what doesn't? Well, who knows?... We're tiptoeing into subjective territory here, and it's a minefield to be sure. Therefore, what follows is simply my personal discourse about prayer and how prayer manifests itself in my work as a filmmaker.

Fade In.

Sssssh. Keep it down. Stop talking. Put a lid on it. Or the ever popular — *just shut up.*

For me, the simple but always difficult task of listening is step one in prayer. Listening involves the declaration that what surrounds us may be at times more important than self. From the personal to the social and political, listening can take many forms: a friend asks for advice, an adversary issues a threat, a woman weeps, a daughter cries, an entire race of people cries out for freedom, or sadistic bellowing people claim that "God is on their side" minutes before they unleash cruise missiles into a neighborhood — I listen to all of them. And hopefully along the way, they listen to my fears, my anger, and my hopes. I believe that prayer can begin only after I've taken myself out of the equation — and I don't know if I've come across a more difficult task.

For me, step two in prayer is the ongoing act of obliterating the idea that we need to pray to a humanlike sky god (read: Santa Claus) who sits at the right hand of a vending machine. *"Please, Lord, help me hit the home run — win the lottery — get that job — cure Gracie's cancer — kill my enemy, give me this, oh and I want that, too . . . and this over here — Hey, I'm talking to you — this over here might be a nice addition to my pile of useless junk as well."* The vending machine prayer scenario projects our selfish wishes and superstitious fallacies out into the cosmos, and then we anxiously await (and expect) our return package delivered quickly via Federal Express. Judgmental? Well, maybe . . . but for me, the vending machine prayer scenario, the sky god, exists on the same level with Humpty Dumpty and that jolly cow that jumped over the moon. It's human, it's selfish, and it can be insulting. And in extreme cases that seem to happen all too often, this type of sky god prayer can be Draconian and sinister — especially when the "answered prayer" is the go-ahead to shatter dreams and destroy human life.

So here we are on this rock hurtling through the universe — all of us space travelers, all of us looking, searching, and praying for those answers and reasons that will get us through another day.... Can prayer change the world? Can it heal a broken heart? When it seems like a prayer is answered, we rejoice in it; when it seems like a prayer goes unanswered, we fall back on that old safety net saying, "Gracie died of cancer; I guess it was just God's will." Can prayer change the course of human events? Can it help cure Gracie's cancer? Who really knows?

Take one glimpse into the Middle East — prayer is everywhere, plenty of gods to go around, more than enough holy words — and the death march continues, hatred reigns supreme, and blood flows like water ... entrails and blood cutting a path through the "holy land" since who cares to remember. Only a madman would say prayer is working. But maybe it's like the old adage that says you can't say that Christianity has failed because it's never really been tried. Maybe prayer has never really been tried as a true agent of change. Maybe the sky god and vending machine prayer scenario has poisoned the well. Maybe the conviction, "My god is bigger than your god," is an obstacle to prayer, a barrier to change. Maybe we need to reevaluate prayer. Maybe prayer needs to be collective — no flags, no boundaries — human beings putting aside their petty and selfish differences and realizing a shared goal of harmony, peace, and justice, a shared and equal goal that exists in all of us, and if we connected the dots we would create one organism, one people, one world (insert sound effect: a turntable needle is ripped across a vinyl album to an abrupt halt). *Yeah, sure* — and then maybe that aforementioned cow will really jump over the moon. But, hell, we can try, we have to try — what other choice do we have? Nihilism isn't a whole lot of fun. If we care, and we do, we have to try; we have to be prayer revolutionaries blazing new paths, finding new ways to pray in a collective manner, offering communiqués that involve equal parts of ourselves, our planet, and our Creator.

For me, prayers can take on various forms. They can morph from one kind of collective communiqué to another. They have to be different; we're all different as we attempt to suggest change in our own lives, in the lives of loved ones, in the lives of others, in instances where we see poverty, war, hatred, intolerance, injustice, and hopelessness. Now, as prayer revolutionaries, we need to think differently, we need to suggest spiritually organic alternatives to the spiritually stunted Norman Rockwell image of pleas for divine intercession — you know, those cute kids on their knees in nightshirts looking toward the heavens, focused on our infamous sky god with dreams of hitting it big, thanks to the lucky wave of a magic wand. No fuss, no muss — drive-thru repentance and instant change, just like fast food and oatmeal.

Our desires and needs will certainly be different, but the entreaties to follow will require four foundational elements at all times. Number one: the prayer must involve not instant magic, but rather change that entails the understanding of circumstances through education, compassion, and tolerance — a well-thought-out petition. Number two: the prayer cannot be asked when the goal or essence of the prayer is at someone else's expense. Number three: the prayer must be constructed in a collective and unselfish manner — again, equal parts of ourselves, our planet, and our creator. And finally, number four: we must ask for help and acknowledge that we cannot go at it alone. Maybe it's pride, maybe it's stupidity, but we rarely admit to needing help, until of course we're in dire straits. If there's one thing that we as a species have consistently proven since our kinfolk crawled out of that swamp a few million years ago, it's that we all need help — and a lot of it.

As you can probably tell, I was never very good in church. In fact, organized religion grates on my senses. Of course, that's a sweeping generalization but so be it: organized religion (as well as some very unorganized religious movements) continues to tarnish and pervert human history — along with any and all governments and the long chain of ruling-class oligarchies. Add these three together, and we

create a trifecta known as totalitarianism, aptly defined for
our purposes here by historian Arthur M. Schlesinger Jr. —
"a totalitarian regime crushes all autonomous institutions
in its drive to seize the human soul." What better example
could be cited as an obstacle to constructive and collective prayer? A beaten populace isn't very good at anything.
Prayer for a beaten populace lacks education, lacks understanding, lacks collective will, and above all else, prayer for
a beaten people lacks hope. Prayer becomes nothing more
than a sad plea for mercy rather than a true organic movement between joyful souls and their creator, a magnificent
force, which has given them the love and wherewithal to
allow for great change and great triumph. So in this sense,
prayer needs action and action needs prayer. The American
enslavement of human beings is the quintessential example
regarding the marriage of prayer and action. The cry for
freedom from African Americans to their Savior was as loud
and persistent and passionate a collective voice for change
as the world has ever seen. But without the actions of coura-
geous freedom fighters — black and white — the horrors of
slavery would have lasted for God knows how long. Con-
versely, the actions of the many would never have sustained
the onslaught of hate and terror without the incredible spirit
generated and maintained by prayer — sometimes in solitude and sometimes in great and forceful numbers. "Mine
eyes have the seen the glory of the coming of the Lord."

Mark Twain once wrote that we must "find a way to make the lightnings carry our messages." Enter the filmmaker ... and if filmmakers want to use their art form, their medium, and ultimately their power as creators (small "c") to create films (read: prayers) designed to enlighten and suggest necessary change, then they need assume the humbling responsibility of intercessor between God and man — *and that ain't easy.* I know. I've tried. Maybe I've succeeded, maybe I haven't. What I've laid out to this point is what I put myself through when I create a film that I care about, a film where the passion runs high, a film that all of a sudden takes on the dimension of prayer, and therefore for me the film becomes a prayer — a vehicle to communicate the ugliness of racial hatred (*Black & White*, 1988), or the slow destruction of our collective soul (*Hollywood Boulevard*, 1996), or the insanity of war, a nice euphemism for murder (*One Bright Shining Moment*, 2005). All three of these films, my prayers, are collective pleas for audiences to look at how we destroy each other in various ways, suggesting we can do better, we must do better.

A filmmaker with a camera — like a soldier's mother with rosary beads — must find the "lightnings" that will "carry our messages" through the cities, the countryside, to heaven and hell and then back again; messages to ignite change, messages "that involve equal parts of ourselves, our planet, and our Creator." To create the film as prayer, the filmmaker uses various tools at his or her disposal to build the motion picture passion play: the well-researched written word, cinematic images that tell a thousand stories, characters that embody the necessary darkness and light, and then finally the visceral power of music and sound. All of these elements, well choreographed, present the possibility for film as a collective and public prayer. But the possibility rests on one final bedrock rule: that the "lightnings" carry messages founded and nurtured in truth.

Whoa...there's the caveat, the catch, the rub, as they say — because "the truth" is like Jell-O: it's hard to handle. One man's truth is another man's lie. Dr. Martin Luther King Jr. spoke his truth, and it moved mountains. Jim Jones spoke his truth, and it moved a few gallons of Kool-Aid.

In the end, "the truth" shall set us free. And so it is for us "prayer revolutionaries," the relative new kids on the block, idiosyncratic filmmakers, poets, songwriters, graffiti artists, et cetera — using our various art forms as a way to illuminate, as a way to suggest change, as a way to acknowledge that we need help...and finally as a way to pray. So be careful with the truth...for at some point they will see the truth and they will see the lie. You can only fool them for so long. History is littered with the carcasses of fools who deceived the people. Be careful as an intercessor between God and man. Your own soul is on the line. No pressure.

And don't drink the Kool-Aid.

Praying in Between

Nora Gallagher

*The author of celebrated spirituality titles
writes candidly about fretting through prayerful silences....*

I AM OFTEN not sure that what I do could be called
prayer. Probably not. I know that some of what I do
could rightly be called plea bargaining. Or a 911 call.

In my wiser moments, I know that prayer is not like
taking an Advil. The results don't happen right away.

Lately, I have been going to Quaker meetings. Let me
back up: Vincent and I are spending time in New York, an
old dream that has finally come to fruition. A month at a
stretch. We work from there, by the grace of e-mail.

When I am in New York, I don't go to the Episcopal Church, my own denomination, but to the Friends
meeting at Rutherford Place, an old leafy street on the
east side of town, below Gramercy Park. Rutherford Place,
like Gramercy, reminds me of an old New York, an Edith
Wharton New York, when private squares and parks were

fashionable and grand, surrounded by brick mansions with wide verandas or columned porches. The Friends meeting-house is on the corner of Rutherford Place and Fifteenth Street, and the meeting is at 11:00 on Sunday.

I walk across New York, from the west side to the east, in the morning on Sunday, when many New Yorkers look as if they are just arriving home from Saturday night.

"Up early?" I once heard one man say to another in our neighborhood.

"Late," replied the other.

I walk on sidewalks, through the fumes of the subway and the early sound of metal awnings being taken up, over to the old building with cracked stones in its front yard.

It was built to house a lot of people, with two tiers of seating, like theater balconies. No cross, no altar, nothing in the center. Wood white-painted pews. An old man was seated near the front last Sunday, with a cane. People walk in and sit down. Nothing starts the service. It just starts. Unlike Buddhism there is no bell or gong or way to sit. You can sit with your eyes open or closed, shift your feet, cross your legs, go to sleep. I open and close my eyes. When I open them, I see the tree outside which I have now seen in spring and in fall.

In the early half of the hour of silence, I am usually fret-ting. Did I actually pay the Visa bill? Should I buy a small Cuisinart for the apartment, or is that a waste of money? Why can't I figure out a way to speak to my mother that is less defensive? Will my new book be a bestseller? Fifteen minutes have gone by. The tree has leaves the color of deep goldenrod.

"I am trying to learn yellow," Van Gogh wrote to his brother, Theo. "It refuses me."

I wonder, to myself, whether I will ever get this, whether I will be able to sit like that old man over there, his eyes closed. If Van Gogh learned yellow (and he did), then I can learn this.

After we have been there half an hour, a man stands up. He clears his throat.

"I have been thinking today," he says, "about Jesus on the road to Emmaus. You know the story. The two disciples are walking out of Jerusalem after the Crucifixion. Traumatized. And this stranger joins them. It's Jesus, but they don't know that. I have been thinking about what it must have been like for Jesus, to have them telling him about himself."

I like this. This idea of Jesus walking, hearing his own story, told to him, the story of his death and his life. I have never thought of this before. I live on that idea for the next fifteen minutes or so, maybe ten, to be more honest. Or five. Then my brain returns to fret mode: Have I made United Airlines Premier status yet?

Then the old man gets up. He says, simply, "I have been thinking about truth. I have been thinking we are a body waiting for truth." He says more, but that is the line that sits with me.

We are a body waiting for truth.

I am a body waiting for truth.

In the last few minutes, before the Quaker children come in from their Sunday school, sometimes it happens, a sudden heading into the deep end, and the symmetry at the heart of the world shows itself just for a second, the way a whale breaches in the water; the shiny, dark, barnacled skin rises up and then disappears. Just for a second. Usually not, usually the children come in, and I am irritated at the disruption and also attracted to their faces. And then it is over. The man behind me leans over a few pews to shake my hand, in silence. Then I am out the door.

But every now and then, days afterward, the smallest piece of the puzzle falls into place.

In the Dry Arroyos of the Badlands

ROBERT W. TWO BULLS

A Lakota way of prayer.

M Y LAKOTA ANCESTORS were deeply spiritual and religious people. Almost everything they did daily was connected to the spiritual realm. If they went out for a hunt, there was usually a great ceremony around it. Special songs and prayers were used to ensure a successful hunt. When an animal was brought down the hunter would give thanks to the animal spirit as well as to the creator for providing the people with food.

When I was still living in South Dakota I used to hunt quite frequently during the fall and winter. The second time I killed a large white-tailed buck I remembered to give thanks to the animal spirit and to God the creator for the food that this animal had provided. I found that this practice had given me a sense of balance within the created order of life. Since I have been living in major metropolitan areas for the last nineteen years I have not hunted any animal. Traveling the great distance home just to hunt has always been cost-prohibitive, and I have had no desire to hunt locally, though I miss it. Hunting deer was just part of the whole experience because most times we would not kill anything and disappointment was minimal. I am sure now the principal reason for this short-lived feeling had much to do with the time spent walking out into the Badlands and surrounding countryside. It was a time of prayer.

The usual routine was to roll out before sunrise and drive with my dad, an uncle, cousins, and brothers far into the countryside until the road faded into the tall, sweet-smelling prairie grass. At this point we would begin walking further into the back country and Badlands. Worrying that we might spook the deer, we rarely utter a word to one another. By this time the sun is breaking the eastern horizon and the air is silent and crisp. We walk all morning along the lip overlooking the lunar-landscaped Badlands. I enjoy seeing up close the varying red pastel hues of each layer of clay that make up this unique formation. Sometimes the pungent scent of the loamy clay soil greets our noses. The air is getting warmer and is filled with the occasional chirp of a bird or screech of a hawk gliding somewhere overhead.

We begin our journey down the steep embankment into the dry arroyos of the badlands. I try to not think of the hard climb that is required upon our return back to our parked vehicle. We walk into an arroyo — the banks on each side are almost vertical and sharp. The path meanders before us.

I begin to imagine how the water runs quickly in torrents, especially after a mighty spring or summer shower. Fortunately, on these days the floor is dry. Sometimes I catch glimpses of fossilized sea shells and other nameless crustaceans from another period of time. They barely protrude from the crusted surface, begging to be picked up out of the dried earth. I realize I am the first human to ever lay eyes on something that was once alive but is now fossilized. I wonder if this is what my Lakota ancestors meant about rocks being alive. I leave them where they lie and where they will remain for another millennium.

I sometimes will stop to sit and look around, picking a few leaves from the sage plant nearby. I take in this plant's sweet-sour aroma, down into my heart and through my mind. I understand why this plant is considered sacred by my people. I look again at the layers of crusted clay soil: it is hard to imagine that this area was once a gigantic sea. I watch an ant slowly crawling in a zigzag pattern across the earth under this fall light. The sun is setting, the air is still and quiet. It is time to wander back to our parked vehicle. The climb back up the steep embankment seems more arduous, especially after a long day of walking. The setting sun casts long shadows over the Badlands below us. Soon it will be dark, the coyote will sing its lonely song, and the land will again be left alone.

I am reminded of a story told to me by the late Reverend Leo American Horse who served as a deacon on the Pine

Ridge Reservation for many years. He told me about a time when he was boy and he was with his parents attending a monthly gathering of some of the churches on Pine Ridge. These meetings were a time to go over budgets and other church business matters. The meeting began on Friday and lasted through the weekend. When they were not meeting they would break for meals, fellowship, and worship. Leo said he remembers once when they all gathered for an evening prayer service just about the time the sun started setting in the west. At some point during the service he happened to look up and saw on top of the hill an elderly Lakota man praying, looking toward the setting sun with hands outstretched. Leo always remembered this because this man was praying in the traditional way while everyone else was using a prayer book. It was symbolic of the parallels and similarities of both the church and traditional Lakota spirituality that was coming together in a good way. How long would it last?

Sometime in my early twenties, about the time I started to attend church regularly, I began to have an active prayer life. I can mark my active prayer life on that day when I turned my will and life over to God, my higher power. I did this under the lifesaving help of the Twelve Steps of Narcotics and Alcoholics Anonymous. The prayers were simple and ones I have used ever since. I pray, when I am in need of strength and courage, "Help me, God." Every night before slipping off to slumber, my wife and I say together the Serenity Prayer:

> *God grant me the serenity*
> *to accept the things I cannot change*
> *the courage to change the things I can*
> *and the wisdom to know the difference.*

I continue praying, keeping it simple and always remembering that God has given me a new day to live. When I was caught in the throes of addiction, I abused my life by taking it for granted. I thought because I was young I would live on. Meanwhile, many of my relatives were dying and their deaths were connected with alcohol and substance abuse. One morning I woke up, realizing that my number might be next. That is when I asked God for help.

Today my daily morning ritual when I awaken is to say the simple prayer, "Help me, God. Give to me the strength and courage to do your will in all that I do today, Amen." Then I drink a little water, giving God thanks for the new day. This was a ritual that many of my Lakota ancestors practiced in the mornings. Some would even enter into the *Inipi*, or sweat lodge, every morning to say their prayers and chant their songs. Not only were they cleansing their bodies, they were clearing their hearts and minds as well. I dream of one day living in the country and being able to make this my morning routine.

How I Pray

MARTIN E. MARTY

*An elder statesman of religion in America
offers a meditation upon prayer — both informal and formal.*

$\mathcal{E}$ VERY MORNING at 4:44 my two alarms awaken me. Following the counsel of good Dr. Martin Luther, this Lutheran makes the sign of the cross, recalling his baptism (and thus repenting), being thus "born again," as we are each day — Romans chapter six — and free for the day. Yesterday with its guilt and burdens and messes is gone. Today we are part of the New Creation. Tomorrow and its worries are not to exist. At least that is how it is all supposed to work, and all things being equal as they some days are, it works.

After shaving I "do" a Moravian devotion, from a devotional book that keeps issuing itself every year. John Wesley was brought up on it (*Losungen*), and Dietrich Bonhoeffer used it at his subversive seminary. It is quaint, almost cornball in appearance. The Moravians choose a one-verse text from each of the two Testaments, intersperse them with two old-fashioned hymn verses, and end with a forgettable prayer. In their randomness they belong to the day and speak to me. I would not try to peddle the book at a megachurch, but at the fireside my "church" is rather intimate.

Four newspapers will have bounced onto the porch, and an hour later Harriet comes down and we read them together, commenting on a world that stands in need of prayer, as do we.

During the day: how do I pray?

Frankly, I've never been the sort who follows the counsels to fall on my knees, set aside times for prayer, and the like. I doubt if I've prayed on my knees, in private, since my confirmation day, May 11, 1941. I am not bragging or complaining, just explaining. I may admire people who do, but I am not good at it. My mind wanders. (I can't meditate, I fall asleep.) *Unless* I am at a retreat, in a company of fellow pray-ers. Then it becomes especially meaningful.

What does daily prayer look like, then? Professor Don Capps of Princeton Theological Seminary wrote a piece, now fugitive for me, that had an angle: think of prayer as continual communication with God. Once my faith has given me a sense that I am not alone in the universe, that there is a Thou — Buber says, "God is to be addressed more than expressed" — it makes sense to picture some sort of communication. Capps compared it to a child, whose "petition" for something extravagant fit into a way of life. Christians like to think that "Thy will be done" is the best and final prayer. In effect, it often comes across: "God, I want my way. But you're bigger than I am. We've been in a contest. You won. So, I guess, 'Thy will be done.'" Capps notices that in the Garden of Gethsemane the night before his death, Jesus wanted the cup of suffering removed, and prayed, "Thy will be done." But he did not throw in the towel. The cup remained before him, *but he kept on praying*, in one of the Gospel accounts.

So I like to think that as I move about, listening to classical music in a traffic jam, being with friends, being befriended, I am in that constant communication with the Other, the Presence — not in a spooky way, but still in a realistic one.

I have been taught by those in the Jewish tradition to think of my study as prayer. I like to say, as I did to Henri Nouwen, that I am a hitchhiker. I read prayerful and devotionally profound poets and prophets, and ride along.

We often have a candle lit, and spouse and I talk about people in need, remembering them, being thankful for mercies, commending the suffering to God. I guess that's a form of prayer.

And I tumble into bed, forgiven and forgetful, usually too ready for sleep to remember to make that sign of the cross for evening prayer.

How do I pray? I accented my "minority" form of prayer: isolated, individual, lonely, private, one-on-One. That is very much the lesser in my book and way.

My prayer is heightened in community. I love "the hours," at retreats, when visiting monasteries, where Christians in parishes set aside a time for a bit of chant and psalm and candle and, *then*, prayer. For me, a climax of worship is the *omnium gatherum* prayer of the community, be it the Eucharistic prayer, the Litany, what is often called "the pastoral prayer," and certainly the intercessory prayer.

From the theologian-ethicist William May I learned to think of intercessory prayer as a climax of worship. Fulfilled and fulfilling intercessory prayer is very public:

- No need or call of anyone present is too trivial to bring to the mind of the community en route to the mind of God. Susie's marriage, Tom's venturing to college, Maria in armed services, Aunt Esther and her cancer, the Johnsons celebrating their baby: these are all made public.

- Second, such prayer lifts the invisibles to visibility. Someone has called intercessory prayer "loving one's neighbor on your knees." You commit yourself to leaving the sanctuary and identifying with others, committing yourself. This is the moment when the homeless, the people who live in culverts and under bridges, abused children, the hungry, those dying in hospices, all get envisioned, remembered, with their needs transmitted through our voices.

- And, third, completed prayer includes prayer for the enemy. That's basic in Jesus' commendations of prayer and worship.

So, simply: in private I pray in "constant informal communication" and in public I pray in "communal formal communication."

And the prayers all end: Amen.

¡Qué lista la Virgen!

Lydia Lopez

An advocate for the poor
offers the prayerful example of the Virgin of Guadalupe.

IT IS THE SIXTEENTH CENTURY. Indians are demoralized by the routing of their gods. Millions of Indians are dying from the plague of Europe.

The Virgin Mary appears pacing on a hillside to an Indian named Juan Diego —

His Christian name.

He doesn't understand Spanish, so she speaks to him in Nahuatl.

He hears beautiful music. *¡Qué bonita la música!*

It is December 1531.

Her dress is covered with Aztec symbols and the Aztec sash of a pregnant woman.

To one like Juan Diego, Mary's attire communicates a powerful message.

Her rich blue mantle speaks of royalty, while the gold stars emblazoned on it signal prophecies of a dying civilization that will soon experience a new birth.

She wears both a Christian cross (on her brooch) and an Aztec cross (centered on her womb)

Her splendor is greater than the sun which frames her, a symbol of the Aztec deity.

At the Virgin's request, this Indian must go several times to the bishop of Mexico City to ask that a chapel be built on Tepeyac (the nearby hill) in her honor.

Juan Diego visits the Spanish bishop.

The bishop is skeptical.

The Virgin tells Juan Diego to climb the hill and gather a sheaf of roses as proof for the bishop.

He finds Castilian roses — among Tepeyac's native cacti. Impossible to find in Mexico in December 1531.

Juan carries the roses in the folds of his cloak, his tilma, a pregnant messenger.

Upon entering the bishop's presence, Juan parts his cloak, the roses tumble, the bishop falls to his knees as he sees the picture of Guadalupe.

That same tilma is today enshrined in the Basilica of Our Lady of Guadalupe at the foot of Tepeyac in Mexico City.

The legend concludes with a concession to humanity — proof more durable than roses — the imprint of the Virgin's image upon the cloak of Juan Diego.

The Virgin chose the brown-faced Mary — *Mi Madre, La Morena.*

All elements spoke directly to the Indian.

The image of Our Lady of Guadalupe (Mexicans call her La Morenita) has become the unofficial flag of Mexicans.

La Morenita is at the center of the Mexican soul.

The Virgin appears everywhere in Mexico; on dashboards and calendars, on playing cards, on lampshades and cigar boxes, even tattooed upon the very skins of Mexicans.

She has become more vivid with time, developing in her replication from earthy shades of melon, Aztec orange, as Richard Rodriguez said, to bubblegum pink.

Cesar Chavez carried the Virgin of Guadalupe in the front of his march for social justice for the farm worker.

Every December 12 in Mexico feels like a religious Woodstock. I tried getting near the Basilica recently, but I had to make my way past 7 million others who had the same idea.

In La Virgen I see myself, the first mestiza, the original Chicana, and because she crosses so many borders I call her the undocumented virgin, the virgin of many immigrations.

I pray to her in specific ways and in general ways. Sometimes as I look at what is happening to her children, mostly Mexicans and Latinos, I just ask for care for them. The journey to get to her for many immigrants is so treacherous and can be so dangerous that I just ask for special care. Her story is of such love and concern that it seems like the most natural thing to do. She came to Juan Diego and said, "Do this not for me but so that people will know that I love them." This is another expression of God's love.

I pray to Jesus, of course. I thank Jesus every moment of my life for the ability to be of service, to be able to help people, to rejoice in this life that God has given me, but I also know that there's a range of expressions of God's care for us. I can say, "Look, I've got brown skin like she has," and that is a wonderful connection God has made for me. She's a place where I can stake my identity. She's *a* way to God, but she's not *the* Way.

It feels to me she is a different person than Mary the Mother of God. To me Mary is too pure, too white, and too antiseptic. There are many different expressions of Mary. There is a Mary in almost every continent, which may mean that the incarnation is coming from a deeper place. Our relationship with Guadalupe is seen in a different dynamic than the one in which we see Jesus or St. Paul or St. Francis; it's this loving mother. I feel that with Guadalupe there's a strong bond I can make — just seeing her and telling her story over and over. Nothing defined; it just happened.

Praying gives me hope, optimism. It is a way of lifting my burdens and saying, "This is happening, and I just want to take some time out to recognize the difficulty and ask for help as I go through this tough spot."

Praying helps me to keep all those cares in front of me. No matter what, it's going to be okay. I tend to be optimistic, to work very hard to solve problems, to try to open doors for people, to help them make connections, all that comes out of that same place — this open, generous, wonderful, inclusive love that has been provided for us, and that we see in the story of the Virgin of Guadalupe.

> *O Virgencita, La Morenita*
> *Te pido tu ayuda*

The Day the Tank Arrived

PAT MCCAUGHAN

A journalist who covers our "hurt and broken world"
reports on prayer and the power of the pen.

THE DAY the U.S. Army tank opened fire on our neighborhood began like most July days in Detroit, sticky and humid, with a limp-noodle kind of feel.

We were several days into the riot of 1967 or, as we would later rename it, the revolt. What had begun as a police raid on an after-hours joint a few blocks away had quickly turned brutal and violent.

Much, much later, experts — from social scientists to politicians — would say the revolt was sparked by pent-up rage over any number of social issues — police brutality, economic disadvantages, lack of access to education and the political process, racism.

I was in junior high school and unaware of rage or economic disadvantage. I did know of racism, although my parents sought to protect us from it over the supper table by using such code words as: "the 'W' fella who said something objectionable." And, "the 'C' fella who responded." Another favorite code phrase of theirs was "the other club." We belonged to one club and "they" belonged to the other.

Their aim was idealistic and laudable, even if impossible; their protection admittedly limited. They planned to rear God-fearing, open-minded, prejudice-free children prepared to work twice as hard in order to gain half as much. Fortunately, they didn't believe it to be all that difficult a task for my four sisters and me. Or so they told us, often and with passion, along with other life lessons.

Endurance was another lesson we acquired in these sessions: life was hard and we should have no expectations of anyone taking time to help us, so we had to be prepared to tough it out, alone if necessary, no matter what. Whatever they were selling, my sisters and I weren't buying. We pretty much had it all figured out already, or so we thought.

Our neighborhood had protected us. It was, to my childish eyes, wonderful and magical. We lived in the heart of the city, within walking distance of its cultural center and art museums, three blocks from where Berry Gordy began Motown Records and just down the street from where Aretha Franklin grew up. We could feel its pulse. We moved inside its rhythmic beat. And we loved it.

There was a carnival atmosphere as this particular day dawned sultry and brooding, overcast. The stench of charred and smoldering buildings filled the air and blocked the sun. The nighttime had been peppered with the sound of distant gunfire and sirens. We inhaled the smoke reluctantly and refused to drink the water, which ran rusty and dark. Had it been poisoned? None of us was willing to risk it to find out.

Inside this surreal backdrop there was familiarity. Our neighborhood had always enjoyed its own diversity — with an Asian family across the street, a Native American family down the block, a Caribbean family, Mexicans, Jews and Arabs, blacks and whites. We were different, and yet there was enough to make us alike; we were neighbors.

I have searched every place I've lived for something like the feeling of being neighbors in that time and place. It meant elder-respect, child-protection, a feeling of being owned by a place and a time, a shared living that went beyond race and face, and none of us desired to move beyond those small borders.

The day the tank arrived we were all outside, watching a steady progression of looters, their cars bowed under the weight of couches and mattresses loaded onto roofs; or on foot, carrying TVs, radios, even six-packs. Sirens screamed intermittently in the background; truckloads of National Guard troopers roared by, wearing combat fatigues, carrying bayoneted rifles, and shouting slurs and catcalls.

We had heard by word of mouth about an alleged radio broadcast telling us to evacuate the area. It was too hot to be indoors. We were lounging outside, adults discussing this rumor over neatly trimmed hedges and calling out to one another across the tree-lined street. Children were jumping rope, playing hide-and-seek. We were all resolute in one regard: we had no intentions of leaving our homes, or our neighborhood, and no one was going to make us, period.

There came a growling, rumbling sound, and we looked up to see a tank, its barrel low to the ground, swing onto the street. Astonished, we froze. For one long moment I was sure the tank had us in its sights. Then we ran for our lives.

The street cleared in seconds. We spent the remainder of the day lying with our faces pressed against the cool tile of our basement floors listening as barrage after barrage of tank fire turned a house around the corner into Swiss cheese. And then, deadly silence.

That day, life lessons came home, including those we heard in church, including those our parents taught. None of it seemed very real before.

Prayer as surrender came home to my heart, and in those moments I began to pray, as St. Paul advises, without ceasing. I prayed in a way I have prayed ever since — cut to the chase, straight from the heart, all muss and no fuss, a child's prayer. A prayer that lasts all day long and into night dreams, with every breath, the prayer that says: God, help us. Help me, God.

I grew up that day. Life lessons were realized along with the shell casings we collected afterward from porches and yards. We sought understanding, explanation in local TV and newspaper reports, to no avail. If we had been killed, would anyone have known what really happened to us?

Eventually, we heard through the grapevine that the tank was seeking snipers. We weren't aware of any snipers in our neighborhood. Afterward, there was no more mention of the tank or the gunfire. We never spoke again about what happened that day.

Finally, I understood why my parents insisted on Sunday church and their hard-knocks lessons to supplement school. I knew, instinctively, in that way you come to understand your name, your very being, that this was war, this was occupation. And we were in the line of fire.

I knew, also, that no one else was going to tell our story. That was the day I decided to become a journalist. It was the day I understood, finally, who God was for me and who I was for God.

Years later, as a reporter covering breaking news for the *Detroit News*, I attended a journalism conference in Florida. Newspapers from all over the country were represented; the conference theme was fairness in coverage. At the opening dinner, in a banquet hall filled with hundreds of guests, we were asked to stand and introduce ourselves by identifying our names and news organizations, and by sharing our first memory of race.

The first woman stood. Although the room was filled with people of every ethnic persuasion, she felt moved to share her first memory of race as being taught that all black people were just "lazy, ignorant niggers."

One by one, journalists whose reporting shaped minds and lives stood, until we reached a colleague from the *Detroit Free Press,* who shared that during the 1967 riot he was told that the black children from the city were going to come into the suburbs and kill him.

In the ensuing years, I have participated in this war that still rages, daily. The names and faces change, from black and Asian, to brown and Arab, to whatever ethnic group du jour, but the goal is the same: to win control of the hearts and minds of people.

I fight, with every weapon available: prayer, the power of the pen and computer, by not giving over ownership of my own mind or soul.

I fight it in my own struggle to overcome my limitations, my prejudices, to not judge, to hold fast to God's unchanging hand, to love. Eventually, that war led me from journalism to the priesthood. I graduated from reporting what people say is truth to dedicating myself to the truth that never changes. It is *the* one story that we desperately need to tell and tell again; to hear and hear some more, in our broken and hurting world.

The story is grace, hope, forgiveness, peace. The story is a God who loves us all immensely through and beyond life. It is my neighborhood revisited, and so much, much more.

I guess I bought what my parents were selling after all.

In a Hospice

LAURA TREISTER

A hospice nurse writes about prayer
from a privileged perspective.

I LIKE TO GO to funerals. I go when I have made a particular relationship with my patient. Or I go when I have made a relationship with the family. And sometimes, I don't really get to know my patient until the funeral. Recently I was sitting in church, at the funeral of a patient who, when I met her, was no longer able to speak. She had had a stroke at the age of eighty-three, and her family was having a hard time accepting her sudden decline and that there was really no aggressive treatment that would be helpful. I sat with them to explain what comfort care meant — that at some point a feeding tube might actually be increasing suffering, that when one's body is slowly shutting down, food is not always a good thing. While we were talking about this at the patient's bedside, the patient herself pulled out her feeding tube. Her daughter and granddaughter, just days before so unable to have this discussion, interpreted this gesture as an affirmation and decided to remove her feeding tube. She died peacefully a few days later. Of course, it doesn't always happen like that.

At her funeral, I learned about my patient as a woman of "unwavering faith," someone who inspired and shared her religious conviction with impressionable young family members and friends in memorable and life-forming ways. In the grief of those who loved and were adjusting to the loss of this powerful woman, I also witnessed their celebration of her "home-going." And I once again noticed the value of faith in providing strength to participate fully in the experience of great sorrow, and thus to move through it.

My patients' families always seem touched that I make the effort to attend the funerals of their loved ones; what they don't know is the personal replenishment I draw from these opportunities. Knowing almost nobody there, I am able to sit alone and inhabit a space that enlarges to hold all the losses I witness and experience. These losses pile up, and I welcome the opportunity to sit and reflect, to receive comfort and strength from being in the presence of these testimonies of faith, and through the rituals of others, to discharge (and thus process and integrate) my own daily grief and loss.

I have wondered — is this how I pray? All my life, I have been pretty much on my own with regard to prayer. While I am comfortable reading along with others in reciting words of formal prayer, I am now aware that my relationship with prayer is more naturally nonverbal — perhaps only because, without any formal training, I have always and unknowingly improvised.

As an innately spiritual and intuitive child born to atheist, skeptical, rationalist parents, I know reality to be variable and ambiguous. Prayer, by definition, holds more than one meaning; it may be a plea for strength in a time of despair, or an expression of gratitude in a moment of joy, or perhaps both. And, as I think about it, this is my experience of that nonverbal place of at once pain and hope.

Sometimes as I sit with families, or as I sit by myself at a funeral, I experience both deep sorrow and pure gratitude to be in this place, to have been welcomed with grace and warmth into families at their most vulnerable and intimately difficult times, to have received that unbelievable gift of being embraced by them when they were embraced by grief, to have been allowed to bear respectful witness to excruciating loss and transcendent celebration.

This is a place I cannot always go by conscious choice, but I'm coming to believe that it is where, and how, I pray.

The Anniversary of Karen's Death

CHESTER TALTON

A husband's prayerful good-bye to his wife.

NOVEMBER 24, 2003, is a date that I will remember. As I write this, one year later, it is the anniversary of Karen's death. We had been married forty years. We were both young when we were married, and it seemed as if we had always known one another. I remember her from the time when she was eight and I was twelve years old. It seemed to me from the first time that I became aware of her that we were destined to be together forever.

We stood together around Karen's hospital bed as she took her last breath. Our children all stood there with me as we watched her life slip away. She still looked alive, and once again she was beautiful. Karen had battled breast cancer for over a year, had become thin, and she looked like a person who was sick. As she lay there now a moment following her death, she was beautiful. We prayed using the

Book of Common Prayer: "Depart, O Christian soul, out of this world."

I had two feelings. The first was a sudden and huge sense of loss such as I had never felt before, and relief at the end of Karen's suffering and our long wait for what I had come to know was inevitable. I had no idea how to go on without her. We had become part of one another.

As we were leaving the church, the funeral director told me he would leave all of the flowers from Karen's service on our front porch. I didn't really pay attention to his words and forgot them immediately. The next morning, as I backed out of my driveway I saw the flowers on our porch with the bright sunlight of the morning shining on them.

My first thought was of the empty tomb and the words of the angel, "He is not here. . . . "

I felt again very close to Karen. It was as if she had slipped through an opening, and that where she was and where I was were very close. I wanted to be where she was and felt a pull in that direction. On reflection I wondered if this is what happens when one spouse dies and the other dies a short time after. I felt very close to the place of death where Karen was.

During the year before Karen died, I had an unusual experience several times — a feeling of being awakened early in the morning by someone taking the end of my foot and shaking it. I would wake up and look around, see no one, only Karen asleep in the bed next to me. The experience was so real, and it happened so many times in the same way, that I told Karen about it. We talked about it. We agreed it was a dream that was recurring because of something that I was dealing with in my life.

About a month after Karen died, I had the dream again. This time as I woke up and looked around I saw a light like an electric charge stretching between two points on Karen's side of the bed. It moved up to the ceiling, and then toward the door which was slightly ajar. Slowly this charge appeared to move out through the open door into what seemed to be a gauzelike substance that lapped through the door like tongues of flame. Then it was over. I was sitting up still watching the door, wondering at this that had happened.

I don't really know if I was awake or asleep, and have come to think that it doesn't matter. What I believe with all my heart is that I was given the privilege of seeing Karen's soul being escorted out of this world. In spite of what I said earlier about feeling that our two worlds had come close, I think that even though Karen had "crossed over," as it were, this was the final departure of her spirit. Since that moment I have had no sadness about Karen's having died. I continue to miss her, and my heart still aches, because we are no longer on the same journey together. What I know for sure is that Karen has moved into God's presence in a different way than I am in God's presence, and God has allowed me to know that.

It is now nearly one year since these things happened. I am firmly back in this world. Time is a healer. I have come to understand that life goes on, as much a cliché as that may sound, and that God has created us to live in this life for as long as we have.

How do I pray? My prayer is always to give thanks to God. To give thanks to God for life, and to give thanks to God for death, for to God they are both alike. Then I pray for faithfulness, that I will be faithful, because God can always be trusted.

Why Do I Go to Church Five Times a Day?

Sister Cintra Pemberton, OSH

Communal prayer in a religious community.

PSALM 62 says: "For God alone my soul in silence waits; from God comes my salvation." This is the prayer in my heart, said over and over, as I sit in the darkened chapel each morning before Matins. The time seems to fly by some days and drag by on others, but it's essential, life-giving time nevertheless. As I sit alone in the silence, sometimes I feel the presence of the angels. I can hear them singing in some faraway place, calling me to join my voice with theirs, and when the time comes later in the day, I will try to do just that.

The bell for chapel rings; the lights come on; I have to shield my eyes against the sudden brightness. I move from my corner to my place in choir; the other sisters come in and take their places; we find the pages in our breviary; the Angelus rings: Hail, Mary, full of grace; God is with you. After the Angelus, we begin Matins: O God, open our lips, and our mouth shall proclaim your praise . . . and the day has begun.

Matins is just the first of the four daily offices for us sisters in the convent. After Matins we always celebrate the Eucharist, and then at noon we come back to chapel for the midday office of Diurnum; at 5:00 we have Vespers, and around bedtime we have Compline. That means we go to church five times every day. Many years ago, when I told one of my friends that, she was shocked. "Five times a day!" she gasped, "What on earth for?" I was taken aback myself — I hadn't thought about it that way — and I really didn't know how to answer. Why do I go to church five times a day? It was a while before I realized that I go not because it does anything for God — God does not need my prayers — but I go because of what it does for *me. I* need my prayers. It's what keeps me sane and balanced, and it's the steady discipline that helps me to grow into the person God created me to be.

I love the rich liturgical diet of the daily office. Besides celebrating the church seasons throughout the year, there are all the saints, major ones and minor ones. Every day is just a little different, so we need an ordo (an order of the day) to guide us. Every office has different readings from scripture, canticles, hymns, and prayers, but always at the heart — what is never different — is the psalms.

There's something mystical about the psalms. When I pray "My God, my God, why have you forsaken me?"

(Psalm 22) every other Friday morning, I am right there with Jesus on the cross, because there are so many times when life is really tough and it's easy to feel abandonment — if not myself, then someone we know and love has been or is now suffering greatly and feels abandoned by God. Then I can remember my family or friends with cancer or the victims of 9/11 or the people of Iraq and pray for them — and I do.

Dozens of the psalms soar in their praise for God — they praise God for the beauty of the earth, for the birds of the air, the fish of the sea, the glory of the sky; dozens of others thank God for great abundance and plenty; others beg God for help or for healing of wounds and hurts; still others rage at God in impotent fury against one's enemies — and who does not at times feel they have enemies — and we are called to pray for them, too. Every human emotion is in the psalms, and when you pray all 150 of them on a two-week cycle, day after day, week after week, year after year, they truly get inside your soul in an indelible and ineradicable way. That's what going to church five times a day does for you, and it changes your life at its deepest level.

Vespers, I think, is my favorite of the monastic offices, probably because we always sing it. Something indescribable happens when we sing the psalms, canticles, hymns, and prayers, but especially when we chant the psalms. We're not trained singers, and it's not that we have particularly good voices — we're just average women with average voices who use our voices to pray. But because the sound is very unself-conscious and natural, sometimes people seem to think we're musically special. We're not. We are just doing our best with our voices to praise God, and God does the rest. We often make mistakes, but that doesn't matter very much. When I stumble, it's usually because my mind has wandered, and I like to think God has gently tapped me on the shoulder and reminded me to come back to prayer.

Praying in the daily office is not like praying in a parish church. We sisters strive to speak or to sing as one voice, to create one single blend of sound. No one speaks or sings faster than a neighbor, because it breaks the unity of sound, and there is no longer prayer in one voice. Nor is there any need for anyone's voice to be particularly loud. In a monastic setting, it is far better to speak or sing quietly and gently — God is not hard of hearing. For most of us, this takes real discipline: no forging ahead, no belting it out — but then no holding back, either. This is a kind of discipline that is life-giving, and we get to practice it five times each day. It's a kind of symbol of community: the more we are able to speak or sing as one voice, the more we are able to love and respect one another.

Singing in a monastic choir is not like singing in a church choir, either. First of all there's no conductor, and there is no sense whatsoever of performance. It's simply human voices praising God. The goal, if one could call it that, is to find a balance between offering and listening. Each person must *offer* enough (i.e., sing loud enough) to be heard by the person on either side, but at the same time, each person must *listen* carefully enough to hear clearly the offering being made by the person on either side. It doesn't help anybody to sit in the choir and simply listen; the choir needs each person's offering. At the same time, if someone's offering is so loud that someone else's offering is drowned out, that's no good, either. Each person needs to listen to everyone else at the same time they are making their own offering. When the balance is exactly right — and often it is — there comes that precious mystical awareness of being surrounded by the angels. No one can ever predict when it will come, but that is what the choir always strives for: the balance that brings perfection and the Holy Spirit.

Of course there's even more than the balance between listening and offering and praying as one voice, because concentration and focus also come into play. If all the sisters sing on "automatic pilot" (and oh, what a pitfall that can be when you've been singing the office for many years!), on the surface it may sound fine, but if minds are somewhere else, that mystical perfection for which we strive will not happen — we won't hear the angels. If I (or anyone else, for that matter) am in turmoil on the inside because I am preoccupied with some project, or if I am at odds with one of my sisters, that mystical perfection will not happen. The same is true for all of us — that's why those moments of mystical perfection are so rare. But when it does all come together, the whole choir knows it, and there emerges an exquisite delicacy, a kind of crystal fragility of sound that one knows instinctively is the presence of God. We are surrounded by the presence of the angels, and our spirits soar — and the praise of God is perfection itself.

So why do I sit quietly in the chapel before Matins each morning? Not only to prepare myself for the coming day, but also to prepare myself for the discipline of the daily office. The discipline of the office strengthens me and nourishes my soul. The discipline of trying to blend my voice with the voices of my sisters reminds me that I am not alone in the Christian walk; others are there with me, trying just as hard as I am to find that mystical balance of listening and offering which leads to true community, which helps me to grow in love. Why do I go to church five times a day? Because I hear the voices of the angels in some faraway place calling me to join with them in praising God; and in the repeated praising of God throughout the day, I grow more fully into the person God has created me to be.

If Prayer Is a Thread

Felice Picano

*A distinguished novelist writes with candor and force
about his relationship with God.*

"PRAYER IS A THREAD," I read somewhere. And while I don't remember the entire quote or where it's from, I assume the thread is between oneself and one's Deity. And the string that is prayer is more or less the communication device.

If that's true, then my own thread is frayed to the point of being quite threadbare, although still not entirely broken. This is why:

I grew up in a fairly moral and ethical family, but without strong specific religious values. During my preteens I began investigating various religions on my own, mostly because of my classmates. But while I flirted with Judaism, I never chose it. By the time I was legal and on my own, I was pretty much a Buddhist, that being for me the religion with the least amount of violent history connected to it. I meditated and did daily yoga.

From the time I was a teenager, however, I was aware that I was in communication or dialogue with a higher being than myself. Whatever I called my co-communicator, Brahma, Buddha-nature, or even the pagan "Genius," it was a dialogue, with me expressing a wish to become fulfilled as a person, and if I could help others along the way, that would be great too.

I'd been blessed with many innate artistic talents, but painting and writing soon pushed performing arts out of the way. My life experiences slowly but surely moved me from art toward writing, so rather than fight the trend, I went with it. But while my first novel written at age twenty-six was remarkable enough that a friend found an interested literary agent, no one wanted to publish it. And it was five years until a second book was bought. During those five years I alternately worked and ate or wrote and starved. So even though I felt I was being moved by a larger hand into writing, that same hand was doing little to ease my way.

Even so I was published at last, and my career and my private life fell into place neatly, and I was soon surrounded by the first social group of my peers I was pleased and proud to be around. I was nominated for literary prizes, I wrote bestsellers, I broke new literary ground with *The Lure,* the first gay novel to be picked up by a book club, and began my own gay publishing company to help other writers. Besides all that, one special man eventually moved into my ken, named Bob Lowe, and soon we were the most important people in each other's lives.

Such a paradise couldn't last, and it didn't. In early 1979, a former housemate of ours at Fire Island Pines fell ill with a series of diseases and died at the end of the year. He's now considered the first AIDS case on the East Coast. By mid-1980, another close friend developed Pneumocystis and CytoMegaloVirus, and quickly died. By mid-1981 Paul Popham and I stood on a boardwalk and traced the lines of illness of the people we so well knew and concluded, in Paul's words, that "It's contagious. We're all dead men!" Paul, Bob, and another dozen friends met and formed what would become the Gay Men's Health Crisis. So the 1980s went on.

By the time the decade ended, I'd lost more than 90 percent of my acquaintances, four of the seven members of the seminal gay writing group, the Violet Quill, most of those close to me, a business partner in Gay Presses of New York, two brothers, their wives, and a child each. Before he died, author-activist Vito Russo said to me, "Sweetie, I'm sorry I've got to go and leave you increasingly alone in this war zone." And that's pretty much what it was — a holocaust, a city after an atomic bomb, a war zone.

But, I kept telling myself, I could handle it. I could wash shit, blood, and urine off friends who'd once been Apollos and who were now a skull atop a stick corpse-body; I could cope with the madness of those who lost their memories and their minds; I could deal with those who raged and those who repented, those who couldn't walk and those who became epileptic and worse; I could ignore an uncaring government and a shell-shocked medical profession that often knew less than I did; I could look away from the spit, foul gas, and the death rattle of a loved one in my arms as he died — because Bob was healthy.

Then Bob displayed symptoms of AIDS and was tested. He lived less than a year, and the first time he was hospitalized he died. Or rather his brain died. His uncomprehending mother insisted on revival despite Do Not Resuscitate signs all over the room and his chart, and when I came the next morning he was brain dead — a body being breathed by a machine. For two weeks I went daily, washed and powdered and shaved that thing, removing all the ridiculous attachments, until only the breathing machine was on. And, since that would sound the alarm if I shut it off, I arranged with my attorney to have her present when I did so.

She was late, and his body died while I was waiting. Before he died though, I held his hand and told him, "If there is an afterlife or reincarnation, I swear I'll find you. This relationship may have lasted sixteen years, but it is by no means over."

At the memorial service at New York's Ethical Culture Center, among friends and colleagues, a dozen people I'd never met told us all how Bob Lowe had enriched and changed their lives. As I left the room last, my friend Susan Modlow tried to calm me, but I told her, "If I live a hundred years, I'll never forgive God for taking Bob Lowe away from me. Never."

The next two years are a blur. The daily dialogue I'd begun decades before was gone from my life, replaced with — nothing. There was little dialogue or communication in my life of any kind, since virtually everyone I'd ever loved was dead. My last close friend in Manhattan died six months after Bob. My aunt told me, "For every door God closes, he opens a window." To which I replied, "But what if I despise everything in that window?" She'd sputtered: "You can-n-n't!" The *hell* I can't. Blackness and despair descended.

On a reading tour for a new book in Los Angeles, I realized that the light that had gone out of my life when Bob died might be brought back in artificially, if I moved. As soon as I could do so, I did move. Before I left, I made sure my last few friends knew where I stood. I still hated God. And I reiterated my position that nothing could ever compensate for my losses. Nothing. Ever. The move was to waste time. Nothing more. I figured three years.

Away from the scene of all that horror, I slowly began to not think of it. There was as much light as I needed in L.A., and I connected with acquaintances from before and made new friends. Nine years later, I found I had to invite fifty people to my sixtieth birthday.

No other compensation arrived. No new companion ever announced himself. I used to speak to a dozen people a day,

to Bob three times a day at work alone; today, if I speak to
a specific person once a week, that's a lot. I write, I read,
I hike, I garden, I visit friends in Orange County, Santa
Barbara, the Desert, and San Francisco regularly. I travel a
lot for work.

People often ask why I'm alone. I tell them my soul mate
died. End of story. I don't elaborate. I don't tell them the
truth: that I've become like the Golden Bowl at the center
of Henry James's novel. Recall that the bridal gift, while
apparently gorgeous and desirable, hides — until one comes
very close — a flaw that runs through it. Pick it up wrong
and it will shatter. That's me, and most men with the right
instincts can recognize it and are warned away.

I never turned bad, but while I do what people call "good"
in the world, I do it quietly, and the real reason I do it is,
let's face it, ego. It's like when my father became ill in 1997.
In the 1960s we'd come to detest each other, and the first
chance I got I walked out of his house at the age of sixteen
and never looked back. But with everyone dead around him,
he was forced to deal with me when he needed help. So I
became the best son possible; so much so that he began to
lie to his friends how I'd always been his favorite — yeah,
sure! Rewrite history.

Only my father and I ever knew that I treated him nobly
to show how superior I was to him; the pretense included
his funeral. In the same way, until now, only God and I
have known why I'm helpful, useful, charitable, generous,

encouraging, positive, and friendly to so many: to show that I'm superior to the contemptible destiny imposed on me.

I'm aware this is what psychologists would call "a very poor attitude for any real reconciliation." But the way I figure it, I'm hardly self-created, am I, and I've spent six decades trying to correct all the many physical, mental, and emotional flaws that arrived *intacta* with this rather shoddy creature: myself. Frankly, I think I've done enough.

Meanwhile I've begun to ask for a safe trip before I travel in my car or on a plane, and I've thus begun some kind of extremely tenuous reconnection to what once connected me so closely to a higher being and to, let's face it, the inner core of myself. So far, it is the most fragile of threads, easily broken, almost not there.

Prayer in Islam

Laila Al-Marayati

*A female Muslim physician
describes the riches of prayer practice in her faith.*

THE DAY BEFORE I left from Amman, Jordan, to enter the West Bank via the Allenby Crossing (controlled by Israel), I prayed with all my heart for God to let me enter. "But, oh Allah," I said, "please let me accept whatever happens as Your will, for certainly You know what is best." After seven hours of waiting, I was shocked to hear the Israeli border police officer yell at me, telling me to go back to Jordan. Was it possible? But I had prayed in earnest! Why didn't God answer my prayer? I so desperately wanted to enter the West Bank on behalf of a humanitarian organization that I represented and so that I could go to the Gaza Strip to visit my relatives who were eagerly waiting for my sister and me to arrive.

But, it wasn't meant to be. God did not will it to be so. Could I accept that? I said that I would; now here was the moment before me. In an expression of deep faith, my cousin who was so disappointed that I wouldn't be coming said simply, *"Alhamdulillah."* All praise and thanks to God.

In other words, as the Qur'an commands us as Muslims, "We hear and we obey." Allah knows what we know not, and believing in that is a key test of faith.

In Islam, prayer takes different forms depending on the circumstances. The most familiar form of Muslim prayer is the ritual that takes place five times a day. We stand, bow, and prostrate ourselves before our Creator. Everything we say during those prayers has been communicated through generations in emulation of Prophet Muhammad, peace be upon him (pbuh).[1] It is a formal process meant to remind us throughout the day of what is important in life. No matter how busy or preoccupied, we stop our involvement in the material world for a few minutes of devotion to God. During the prayer, we recite verses from the Qur'an, praise God Most High, and ask for His blessings on ourselves and previous generations of believers and prophets like Abraham.

At times, during those moments, it is a struggle for me to stay focused, to prevent thoughts of the day's activities from entering my mind: taking the kids to soccer practice, making a phone call regarding a patient, wondering if I have everything I need for an important meeting. Then I remember a saying of the Prophet (pbuh) that advises the believers to pray each prayer as if it is our last prayer. With that in

---

1. An acronym meaning "peace be upon him or her"; usually used in reference to the prophets.

mind, I become conscious of each word and each motion as I fulfill my obligation to my Lord.

Prayer, or *Salat*, is one of the five pillars of Islam. In the Qur'an, believers are described first as those who "establish regular prayer and render the self-purifying dues." Prayer and charity go hand in hand as a pair of actions that manifest our belief and cleanse our souls. Through prayer, we find redemption, forgiveness, love, and the all-encompassing embrace of God. The five daily prayers are acts of submission to God.

Supplication, or *du'a*, is the more personal prayer we engage in throughout the day and throughout our lives as we give thanks, ask for help, and seek refuge. In following the tradition of Prophet Muhammad (pbuh), many Muslims recite a *du'a* upon rising in the morning, before sleeping, at the beginning of a meal, and at the start of a journey. All of the supplications recognize God as the source of life, showering His blessings upon us. We ask for His guidance and pray that He guides us to the straight path, keeping us away from the suffering of Hell.

Another form of prayer in Islam is known as *dhikr*, or remembrance of God. Most Muslims understand this to mean repeating certain phrases a specific number of times, always contemplating the attributes of God. I sometimes recite these to help me fall asleep, or when I'm frightened and uncertain, not knowing what else to do. I find them especially helpful during turbulent airplane rides! We repeat things like *Allahu Akbar* (God is Greatest), *Alhamdulillah* (All praise to God), *Subhanallah* (Glory to God), and *La ilaha illa Allah* (There is no God but God).

It would seem so far that prayer is a one-way conversation from the Believer to God. But when I pray, I always remember the following verses:

> And if My servants ask you about Me—behold I am near; I respond to the call of him who calls, whenever he calls unto Me: let them then respond unto Me, and believe in Me, so that they might follow the right way. (2:186)

> So remember Me and I shall remember you; and be grateful to Me and deny me not. (2:151)

> And as for those who have attained to faith in God and hold fast unto Him — He will enfold them within His grace and bounty, and guide them unto Himself by a straight way. (4:175)

God does respond to our prayers, although sometimes I would feel better if He would just send me His advice in a letter in the mail because I am afraid of missing His signs, wishing the answers would be easy and right in front of me. Usually, when I pray late at night, asking for guidance on something related to work or family, I perform the *istikhara* prayer where I ask that if something is good for me and my faith, to let me be receptive to it, but if it is bad for me and takes me away from my religion, to remove it from me. I will pray *istikhara* before making an important decision.

Some Muslims will see God's reply in a dream. For me, I wait to see how I feel in the morning and then go with my instincts at that moment, trusting that Allah is answering my prayer, guiding me to the straight path. At other times, something will happen the next day that I interpret as a sign favoring one decision or another.

But, in the end, most of my prayers are communicated at random points throughout the day. I seek refuge in God before I lose my temper with my children. I ask God to strengthen me with confidence and ease before I speak before an audience, I thank God for allowing me to witness a spectacular sunset, and I say *alhamdulillah* for an act of unsolicited generosity from one of my sons. Now that I think about it, I realize that I never stop communicating with God on some level every single day. I can't imagine a moment without such an exchange. This, to me, is *taqwa*, or God-consciousness, a continuous state of being for which we continuously are striving.

God's wisdom in His decision that day at the Allenby Crossing becomes clearer all the time, but I still hope — and pray — that He will see fit to enable me to enter the Holy Land again.

Finally
Letting Her Die

James A. Hoyal

*Through prayer, a father confronts
the sudden death of a daughter.*

SHE WAS TWENTY-TWO YEARS OLD, a senior at the University of Tennessee, and just at the beginning of the adventure of doing things for herself, when her life was cut short in an automobile crash on May 10, 1981.

She was doing her student teaching in English at a Knoxville high school when it happened. Many of her students drove the sixty-five miles to Etowah, Tennessee, for the funeral. Several of them told my wife, Peggy, and me things like, "Becky had it all together." You could tell they loved her and were bewildered by such a turn of events.

The funeral service was packed, and long lines of folks came by the night before the funeral to comfort and share our sorrow. The bank in Etowah, where she worked during summers, closed for the afternoon of the funeral. The president told Peggy and me that the bank had not done this before, but Becky was an exception.

At the time I was principal of a local elementary school. The funeral had been on Monday, and though I was brokenhearted, I went back to school the next day, Tuesday. As I walked into the building that morning, I was met by one of our second-grade boys. He didn't know what to say to me, but finally, after a moment or two of hesitation, said, "I suppose you went to the funeral yesterday, didn't you?" I smiled. We high-fived together, and I said, "Yes, I suppose I did." Then the two of us walked down the hall together, arm in arm. I'm sure our contact as we walked down the hall meant much more to me than it did to him. It was good to feel the touch of humanity again after the devastating loss of a child.

A few months after Becky's death, Peggy and another mother, who had lost a son, established a local chapter of the Compassionate Friends, an international organization created as a support group for families who have experienced the loss of a child. Soon I became a part of the group as well.

We met once a month and ministered to some fifty to sixty persons. Discussions with others who were there for the same reason became a true healing environment for many who participated. I began to read everything I could concerning death and the loss of a child. By the second year I had the privilege of holding seminars in East Tennessee concerning the problem of death and its devastating effect on those left behind. This was also a part of my own healing experience.

My major healing, however, came through the presence of God. Though I have spent a lot of my life in the field of education, I am also an ordained minister, serving churches, being a military chaplain on active duty with the U.S. Air Force, and then some twenty more years as an Army National Guard chaplain with the state of Tennessee. When Becky's death came I was well aware that such devastation occurs in this life. As a result, I found no need to be angry with God when my own child was taken. I was brokenhearted but not angry. God had been my God for many years, giving Peggy and me a good life together as well as three children. Our other two, Andy and Anne, are still alive and doing well. Becky was our youngest. We have been blessed along with being devastated at her death.

For the next eighteen months, I struggled in my heart because of our loss. I found prayer to be a genuine help for putting my life together again. I became involved in many things that were helpful, but my nightly prayers were the bedrock of my healing. Since I was not angry with God for our bad fortune, I had no reason not to lean on him for help. And that he was. Each evening I would spend some time in our backyard, where I could look at the stars, the night sky, and occasionally the moon and be reminded of my own frailty as over against the creative world and God. We talked like friends. We talked of Becky. I felt he had taken over my position, so I told him what I hoped for her and reminded him to take care of her. I never heard his voice, but I sensed that he had heard mine and made me feel that I had nothing to be worried about. She was in better hands than mine. I learned much during that year and a half of the goodness and kindness of God. While I was praying in my yard, a lady who lived behind us saw me, called my wife, and said that there was a man in our backyard. She said she had seen me there before and was worried that I might be up to some mischief. Peggy assured her that it was just me and God, no need to worry.

One way God met me was through my dreams. I dreamed of Becky often. One dream was persistent. I saw a large ocean liner docked at an island and knew that Becky was on it. In October 1982, a year and a half after she died, I had a variation on the dream which was very confusing. The same island was again in my dream, but the boat was gone. I felt sadness but also peace. When I woke from the dream I realized that the ocean liner had been a kind of way station, and that I had finally let her die. It was the last dream I ever had of that beautiful island.

Prayer is a conversation with God, yet mostly it is his presence with us, his eternal spirit breaking into time. Prayer is being in the presence of the Father.

A Supernatural Battle

TORY CONNOLLY WALKER

*A woman prays "like a house afire" for release
from the demons of mental illness, alcohol, and drugs.*

I WAS ONCE a radio and part-time television news reporter for several years after graduation from Ohio
State University — working in Columbus, Ohio. But one
fine day I jumped a smoking jet to L.A. when I became
bored with my "dreary little town."

It was 1983. I was twenty-seven years old, and no reporting jobs were immediately available during my impatient
California work search. Curiously, when a tantalizing offer
in the music industry was given to me through the friend of
a friend, I had no problem making a dramatic career switch.

Suddenly I found myself working as an assistant man-
ager at Motown Hitsville Studios in Los Angeles. It seemed
to be the emerald gate to "Excitement City." Songwriting
was something I did semiprofessionally, and I loved music
even more than I loved news — so I thought I had died
and gone to job heaven. Lionel Richie, Smokey Robinson,
Jermaine Jackson, Rick James, and Stevie Wonder — all casually walked through the studios or sat at a desk across

from mine, making small talk and telling jokes. It seemed I laughed all day long.

Spiritually for me it was anything goes. After work, I dabbled in Hinduism, did Buddhist chants, read the Koran, and practiced metaphysics while attending the Church of Religious Science. Did I mention I became confused? My rarely opened copy of the Holy Bible gathered several layers of dust as I went looking for Jesus and His "lost years" in esoteric texts, but didn't find anything. On the job I continued working on the *Motown 25* television special. It was a grand and giddy time.

Moving toward another level of my game to combine journalism and the music business (I intended to write an article on the television special while working on it) I was blindsided as if opening the door to a nightmare world. . . . Boom! I fell into a frightening abyss. I began to hear voices, see people's faces change, and heard and felt demons whizzing past me uttering garbled curses.

I never made it to the Pasadena Civic Auditorium to watch the *Motown 25* special — the program I had worked on — from a coveted seat. Instead I was spirited away by my mother on a fast and spooky jet to a mental hospital, a world away in Cincinnati, Ohio. I was terrified just looking at the walls. Six weeks later the taped version of *Motown 25* came on national TV. I stared forlornly at the television set in the dayroom of the mental hospital in smiley-face green foam slippers, while Michael Jackson made music history with his "Billy Jean" song-and-dance spectacle that shot his career into the stratosphere.

"I worked on that show," I said weakly. No one heard. I was diagnosed as manic depressive.

For a total of twelve years, racking up a tally of twenty-two agonizing times, I was admitted into an unholy-go-round of psych wards. I had been prescribed enough drugs to "kill a horse," as my Aunt Marian would say. Sometimes Haldol, Mellaril, Lithium, Thorazine, and Elavil — all at once. Then for another several years I struggled with vicious alcohol, cocaine, and finally crack addictions.

How did I think I would escape this thing called mental illness, this horrible Thief of Time and Destination — when my beloved father, "Q.A.," had lost his entire career as a popular junior high school science teacher and his marriage to my mother and his chance to be with me consistently, because of paranoid schizophrenia? The medical field calls it genetics, the Bible calls it generational curses of lunacy. My most effective doctor, Jesus Christ, would whisper His prescription in my spirit, pointing to Matthew 17:21. "This kind (of demon) goeth not out but by prayer and fasting."

Instead of following the Lord's advice, through disbelief, rebellion, and frustration I gave up and was sucked into an underworld of hustlers, gangsters, con artists, and drunks. I was the main drunk. My first husband was a Vietnam veteran and photographer who was angry at the planet for what he suffered in the war. He soon came and went. I continued to suffer from mental illness.

The 1990s were upon me. One bright spot on the horizon was that I met a tall, handsome, and talented man named Geno, with whom I had deep intellectual conversations and who made me laugh. We traveled to Las Vegas to get married immediately. But we both grappled with who God really is — and our personal struggles tore us apart after only a year together.

I began to read my Bible, searching for answers night and day. "Lord!" I cried, "If you freed Mary Magdalene of seven demons, couldn't you free me?!" My Bible fell open to "this kind goeth not out, but by prayer and fasting."

As a news reporter, I had been taught to be skeptical and report only what I had seen. But I can testify there is an active teeming world of real angels and real demons just beyond the realm of sight. Not until I had a supernatural battle with an entity that attacked me on several occasions, and once sent me shrieking in terror as its force shot up my spine, clawed and catapulted me to my knees, did I begin to believe that the paranormal is NOT normal, but oh, brother, is it real.

I had had it. I accepted Christ as Savior and Lord of my life. I went to church and read the Bible. I fasted and I prayed like a house afire. I called a prayer partner I have never met. He said, "Lady, you're going to stop singing the blues!" Then he prayed for the Lord to deliver me. That afternoon, on Ash Wednesday, February 25, 1998, I got down on my knees in a cold and deserted New York City park and prayed for the Lord to free me — from manic depression, alcohol, and drugs. I walked out of that park a free woman. I take no medication and haven't been prescribed any in many years. In December 2002, my husband Geno and I were reunited — after not seeing each other for almost nine years.

My deliverance is a miracle. My testimony is true. The power of prayer unto the Lord Jesus Christ set me free. I have been free from that Ash Wednesday day to this, as I minister to others. God's love is astounding. And oh, His grace is amazing.

An Immigrant in America Prays

RAVI GUNEWARDENA

Prayer is something this Sri Lankan immigrant
is still trying to sort out.

PRAYER FOR ME has been shaped by various influences as I have matured, and it has evolved into something quite different from what it appeared to be at the start. Born into a Roman Catholic family in Sri Lanka I spent the first half of my life unquestioningly practicing the religion of my family by tradition. My childhood recollections are filled with countless hours in church, kneeling next to my mother, praying through the holidays and festivals of the cyclical liturgical calendar, reciting prayers that were taught to me, lost in the repetition of their chantlike form.

In Sri Lanka, because of its multiethnic and multicultural population, one was exposed to several religions, if even only marginally. The pilgrim shrine of St. Anthony was located across the street from the Hindu Temple near the port of Colombo. The Roman Catholic cathedral was not far from a brightly painted mosque. Muslims, Hindus, and Buddhists brought special treats to their neighbors during holidays. I fell asleep to the then-eerie sound of Buddhist chanting coming from the temple up the street.

Living in America since I was eight, I grew to realize that I was culturally different from neighbors and other children at school. Even though we often celebrated the same holidays, my family had different traditions and ate different foods for those events. In a way, being an immigrant in America has enabled my spiritual discovery. While immigration, particularly to Western nations, affords one the opportunity to break loose of traditions that are often held in place by closely knit homogenous communities in the country of origin, it can be viewed by some as a catalyst for the loss of culture, especially by parents who lose control of their children's social and cultural direction. I often wonder what my own parents feel about the various religious paths that their seven children have taken — adopting Anglicanism, Protestant Fundamentalism, Native American Spiritualism, and Buddhism.

I'm comforted to know that displaced immigrants are not the only ones to venture away from the traditions of their upbringing and delve into other belief systems. Thomas Merton, the Trappist monk and theologian who traveled throughout Asia and other parts of the world in order to gain a personal understanding of diverse religions, helped me develop a sense of curiosity (and pride) at a stage that I was trying to reconcile my foreignness with my American social environment. The work of people like Joseph Campbell or my family friend Father Flavian Willathgamuwa and the Venerable Havenpola Ratanasara Thera helped me realize that what religions have in common is more important than what separates them. Swami Nityananda and Devayani introduced me to meditation, chanting, and the Hindu understanding of the many facets of God. Yacoub and Seema, whose families have shown me true Palestinian hospitality, by their graciousness and integrity remind me of the perseverance of faith in a better world while challenging other people's stereotypes.

Prayer is something I am still trying to sort out. Yet I continue to pray, probably in less conventional ways, but for many of the same things for which others pray.

I pray for release from the arrogance that one's own set of beliefs is the only truth that must be imposed on others.

I pray for humility and clarity to understand that by simply making declarations, one cannot presume to "know" God, to know that God does or does not exist, or know that "God is on our side."

I pray for receptiveness to learn the many different forms and names of God, as well as for the ability to see that the phenomenon that one calls God may not be named as such by another.

I pray for the continued struggle to overcome prejudice, to be able to accord humanity not only to those who share one's background and beliefs but to those who don't as well.

I pray for wisdom to realize that imperfection and some amount of suffering are also a part of life; and I pray for compassion toward we who yet struggle to find our way in the world.

I pray for peace, for increasing harmony among people who hold each other as enemies — even sometimes in the name of God.

I pray for my Palestinian brother Yacoub: that he and his family may one day be able to truly return home. I pray for my Israeli sister Sharon: that she will feel safe enough to share the land she calls home. I pray for my Sinhala and Tamil cousins — that they will work toward peace with each other. I pray for all who fear the other: that those who are in power will see humanity in those who are at their mercy.

At times I seek release from all concerns above in meditation, perhaps not even a form of prayer. I sit silently with my eyes shut and try not to engage in the stream of conscious activity that flows through my head. I yearn to know that absolute silence that comes from detachment of all things worldly, from letting go of self and from the craving and scheming that accompany that notion of self, just being. I find this goal the most difficult to accomplish, and yet the glimpses of the experience are most liberating. Could this be the ultimate experience of God, finding the nothingness that is within?

Confessions of an AIDS Activist

TED KARPF

A worker for the World Health Organization
ruminates on prayer, hope ... and helplessness.

I'M NOT SURE that I have ever prayed about HIV/AIDS, but I've lived through it. I am an AIDS activist. It is difficult to remember a time without AIDS. It's all I've ever seemed to know. Every aspect of my personal and professional life since 1983 has been dominated by this damned disease.

We pray by hoping. I suppose this is so. For me, it began with Jerome, who only asked, "May I die in your church?" Every waking moment since I have been dragged kicking and screaming into that place where I could do nothing but say "yes." I've thought of it as surfing a tidal wave. I've heard the roar of the wave for years and am still holding on for dear life. To let go is to fall into the abyss ... of the inestimable mystery of God and know the chaos of death.

At home, the disease seemed to abate through advanced medical breakthroughs and access to care for some, and I thought my work had finished. Then I found my way to southern Africa where the pandemic is out of control, and my heart was ripped open again. The impact of millions of abandoned and ill nearly caused me to fall into the wave. I recall standing helpless on a freezing night in Hlabisa, Zululand. As we circulated the hospital wards overflowing with sick people, with two or more to a cot, the attending physician demanded, "You're a priest. You pray for them!" When I asked why, he replied, "It's all that they have to make it through the night. We have no drugs here." So I prayed by hoping; holding hands, touching the pain, and pleading to the howling wind for help and hope.

Praying by hoping is nothing more than standing in place, riding the wave, and holding on for dear life. I was reminded of my earliest lesson of helplessness by Nesta. Just weeks from her own death, she raised this cry as I held her diseased and shaking body. Weeping over the graves of her dead children and husband she demanded, "Where were you? Where were you?" This question haunts my every moment. I could say nothing, but just hold her.

Likewise I could only hold on and shake with helplessness as 550 HIV+ members of the Treatment Action Campaign shook their empty pillboxes before a government representative in protest for the lack of treatment. These empty boxes signaled hope for treatment to be delivered by their government — treatment that, for too many, will shamefully come too late.

I said nothing, but shook with grief in a trash dump on the outskirts of Umtata, realizing that eighty cents was all that separated the haves from the have-nots: those who would or would not receive the golden drop of Nevirapine at birth. The liberated government of South Africa refused to administer this proven treatment until ordered to do so by the Constitutional Court, years after it was declared safe for newborns. Even so, thirty-seven thousand were born infected last year because of the slowness to respond.

Finally, I shook with fear at the bedside of my life partner watching the infusion of an experimental drug at the National Institutes of Health (NIH) more than a decade ago. I watched helplessly as he shook alternately, with raging fever and then chills, for hours and then for days. And I have held on for dear life as I wakened daily for fourteen years to the shaking of a pill box as he prepared to down this day's first of three or four installments of drugs — "nukes," "non nukes," "protease inhibitors," and pure poison — to ensure another day of life.

Holding on for dear life, I also shake with outrage at my government, which insists on profit in the trafficking of pharmaceuticals, instead of living prophetically, sharing the wealth of our bounty with the 40 million infected, most of whom live in the global South and who also stand waiting in hope.

Scripture informs me that I am a slave to hope. I guess I must be, for I thrill at the notion that basic AIDS treatment has been reduced to a tablet in which three drugs are combined into one, taken only twice daily. I am awestruck at the marvel of technology that has created this new generation of treatment which can cost as little as fifty cents per day, when it used to be hundreds and thousands of dollars per month. Now I am engaged in the effort to bring 3 million into treatment by the close of 2005. I am stuck in the hope of treatment for all.

I am not sure that I have ever prayed about HIV/AIDS. I know only that I have lived it, every day for more than two decades. I have cursed it and damned it and even tried to exorcize it, but I doubt I ever prayed about it. Rather I have prayed with all my heart and all my soul by hoping: Hoping by standing still or standing by; hoping by challenging power and authority; hoping by demanding justice and working for a world with a generation without AIDS, when a child will ask, "What is this AIDS?" Not because his parents have died or her brothers and sisters are dead, but because it is no longer a disease of death. I am reminded of a scriptural text, "Faith is hoping for things not seen" (Hebrews 11:11).

If this can be called prayer, then maybe I have actually prayed about AIDS.

Side Doors Opening

PHYLLIS TICKLE

*A lecturer, author, and authority on religion in America
parses the relationship between creativity and prayer.*

OME FEW YEARS AGO NOW, it became fashionable to
hold seminars and workshops on the interface between spirituality and creativity, most particularly between
creativity and prayer. Unfailingly, my reaction to the an-
nouncement of yet another such event was visceral and
negative. In fact, truth told, once or twice it even became
verbally and unpleasantly so, or that was my judgment of
me at the time. The oddity in this was that I absolutely believe that there is a connection between the acts of either
aesthetic or applied creation and the arts of spiritual practice. The hindrance is that I believe the connection to be
one of geography rather than of substance.

A wise man — although I can no longer remember his
name or where I read his words, I am nonetheless persuaded
by them that he has to have been wise — once observed
that despite our best efforts, we can not define "seven." We
can say what it is in relation to other things, but not in
relation to itself; for being an abstract, seven has no self to

be in relation to. Nor, for the same reasons, can we in any way define even the seven-ness that is seven. Seven-ness, he went on to say, lives in the realm of concepts like prayer or music. Bingo! (It was just here that I perceived the man's wisdom.)

Seven-ness is the stuff of poetry. Or put another way, "seven" has a physical utility of great practical advantage to us, but it also has an intangible life of considerable mystery and beauty. The exact point where the ordinary usefulness of seven morphs into the unknowableness of seven is not clear. We can never locate with precision some moment or place and say of it, "Ah, here, in this spot, seven changes from tool to mystery . . ." for this is, of course, what we are talking about, isn't it? The mystery.

People like me — writers, musicians, painters, philosophers, dancers, etc. — people who make their livelihood out of the intangibles of ideas and metaphors, shapes and colors, sounds and contours, go shopping every day for our supplies in the mall of the conceptual and the mystical. Most of us, I suspect, would say that just as surely as the Greeks spoke of the ideals which precede and appertain to physical objects, so too there is a body that appertains and is subsequent to ideas and abstracts. The trick for us non-physical laborers is to take up residence each day in the realm of the nonlocative and nontemporal and then begin to manipulate what we find there into constructs that we can somehow incarnate and bring out with us each evening as we come home from our labors. That is pure creativity in all its messiness as well as its satisfying glory; but it is not inherently of benefit to the soul, nor is it of necessity prayer simply because its manufacture occurs in the domain of the intangible.

I live now, as I have for almost forty years, under an adapted Benedictine rule of observing the daily offices. What that translates to is that I stop at 6:00 and 9:00 a.m., at noon, at 3:00 p.m. and before retiring to offer the prayers and readings that are appointed for that hour and that day in the church's liturgical year. I enter my breviary or prayer manual as one enters a wayside chapel, keenly aware that I have slipped into another place within the domain of non-temporal, nonlocative being. The words I speak there and the prayers I pray are those that have informed my tradition and its precursors for millennia. They are also the words and prayers that thousands of my fellow Christians are saying with me. Though we speak from our respective physical places within a given time zone, we gather in the words and greet each other in our affection for them. Each time we enter an office, we pick those words up from our fellow Christians in the preceding time zone, murmur them in our hearts, and then set them down again for those who shortly will assume them in the next time zone. Together and in aggregate we know ourselves to be raising a constant cascade of prayer before the throne of God.

Such a regimen is just that, of course... a regimen, a discipline, a way of submitting one's self to the honing and polishing which come from routinized interruption for the sake of gratitude, praise, and adoration. But such a regimen is not sufficient in and of itself to be the sum total of one's prayer life, nor was it ever intended to be. Rather, like any wayside chapel worth its spiritual salt, the daily offices are resting places on the day's highway. They are also, I have discovered, deceptively subtle structures with side doors opening out onto whole parks and vistas of prayer which lie beyond them and at a considerable remove from the highway. Here I enter at least three or four times each day; and here it is that I become, not the creator, but the stuff being created, the material being fashioned. And therein, as they say, lies all the difference.

To Perform with Leonard Bernstein

NORM FREEMAN

A professional musician explains why Carnegie Hall
is a fine place to pray.

I GREW UP UNCHURCHED. My parents did not speak much about God. The three of us never prayed before meals. My religious education amounted to sitting in front of the TV with my father while he watched the occasional Billy Graham crusade. At some point Dad decided he was going to take me to Sunday school at a church no one else in the family ever attended, nor had any intention of attending. His rationale, "going to church as a boy didn't do him any harm," wasn't a compelling vision of faith. I refused the invitation.

For some reason, though, I was drawn to prayer — sometimes waiting for lights out to kneel at bedside, other times hiding under the covers so no one would see me. I had my share of fears, and prayer helped. Praying felt better than not praying. I believed it worked, maybe not right away, but eventually God would make happen what I thought was right.

This seemed fine until fifth grade when my Grandpa Freeman needed bypass surgery. Even after days of lengthy prayer, my grandfather died. God wasn't listening. I was devastated and decided to stop talking to God. Why waste your time talking to someone who doesn't listen? It was years before I returned to formal prayer.

It was about the time of the death of my grandfather that I poured myself into playing the drums. I could spend hours immersed in the care and practice of my instrument. Preparing for lessons and playing along with recordings of legendary performances opened up a new world to me.

In high school I prayed for God to hold my parents' marriage together. God and I seemed to let each other down on that one. A little later I asked for my mom to come safely through some critical surgery. That worked out. God was strange, elusive, sometimes undependable, and yet I couldn't stay away.

After my parents' divorce, I practically moved into the practice room. It was both haven and laboratory. If you have a little talent, and spend four to six hours a day doing something you love, things start to happen. People noticed my progress and dedication. They encouraged me to attend a music conservatory upon graduation from high school. I decided to go for it — four auditions, one a "safe school," three others, each a little more of a stretch than the other. Surprise! You've been accepted to Juilliard.

For a young artist, your major teacher is it. Their interest, involvement, and example open a pathway into the future, bridging the gap between reality and one's dreams. Buster Bailey, a member of the New York Philharmonic and known as the best snare drummer in the world, became my mentor. Buster had the biggest smile. He loved the circus and big bands. He had large, fleshy hands that were powerful and sensitive, capable of producing lyrical and swinging phrases. Percussionists wanted what Buster had, and he freely gave it away with unparalleled generosity and encouragement.

That first year was filled with discoveries. Professors, passionate about the performing arts, introduced us to composers and compositions that stretched our musical vocabularies. It all came together on Monday and Thursday mornings when we met for orchestra. These were amazing ensembles, playing with the unbridled fire of youth. Sitting in an orchestra's midst, a wall of sound washes over, sweeping you into a current of notes, where a confluence of notions, ideas, and insights merge, if you're attuned to listen for them.

At year's end, I received word that Saul Goodman had an opening in his schedule and I could study with him. Mr. Goodman was the timpanist with the Philharmonic for forty-plus years, he taught Buster, and he was a legend. With Buster's blessings, I took the next step.

Mr. Goodman was five feet two inches tall, strong, passionate, and charismatic, possessing an inner spirit that gave birth to the ideas and visions of the conductors with whom he worked: Bernstein, Toscanini, Leinsdorf. If you stood by him when he played, you could feel the energy and music bursting out.

Mr. Goodman taught by example. We knew all his recordings and copied his every move. We were the next generation of disciples. He never tired of demanding our best effort. I vividly remember the lesson when he prodded me to reach deep inside myself and find that thing that would fuel the performance, moving the music out of the realm of my head, and birthing the experience into a new dimension — something that came up out of my gut.

After graduation and four years with Mr. Goodman, it was time to take what he taught outside the conservatory. I was launched — immersed in crafting a career, while also strangely drawn to the lure and intrigue of late nights spent hanging out in after-hours clubs. Heading off to the next day's gig often meant trying to hold it together after a long night with little or no rest.

Home one evening, the telephone rang. It was my grandmother. She called to say hello. We were close, but she had never done that before. I always called her. The next day I learned that she died. Family plans came together quickly. There was little time to process what had happened. The day of her burial I rushed off from the gravesite service to get to a rehearsal of Handel's *Messiah*.

The *Messiah* is standard repertoire. I had played it before, never thought much about it, and never contributed much either. This time I decided to put some effort into learning the piece as I was playing with an orchestra and conductor, whom I wanted to impress. During the rehearsal, I sat around waiting for my entrance, dazed from the morning's events.

The "Hallelujah Chorus" opens with its unmistakable strains. I moved to the instrument, distracted by what had happened, saddened by the loss, disappointed and angry with myself for some of the choices I had made over the last several years. Standing behind the timpani, beating out precise rhythms in unison with the trumpets, tears began to fill my eyes. I didn't feel alone or sorry for myself. I felt connected.

The music was working on me. I remember the exact spot where God really got my attention. It was the verse "The kingdoms of this world are become the kingdoms of our Lord, and of His Christ: and He shall reign forever and ever" (Rev. 11:15). This was when I was overwhelmed by a sense that my grandmother was OK, she understood my sorrow and regret, and the One who rules this world, God made manifest in Handel's "Hallelujah Chorus," was watching over her and watching over me, too. It was going to be OK. This was my penultimate conversion experience. It's not the only one. I wasn't struck holy. God is still working on me. This experience, however, is the one that set me on a radically different course. I made a conscious decision to move toward God. This led me to attempt to learn and understand the ways of God, to start and end my day with prayer, to speak and listen to God often, and regardless of the changing rhythms of life, to return to these patterns and steady habits.

Once I showed up for a dress rehearsal and concert after awakening with the flu. We had rehearsed for days. I didn't think of calling in sick. Besides, it was a rare opportunity to perform with Leonard Bernstein and the New York Philharmonic on the anniversary of his debut with the orchestra at Carnegie Hall. It was an all Bernstein program, plenty of percussion. Mr. Goodman, now retired, would be in the audience.

I had drawn Bernstein's attention during the rehearsals. I wish I meant this in a positive way. I don't. There was a spot in Bernstein's *Serenade* where my entrance on a solo chime note needed to be ever so soft and perfectly coordinated to enter exactly with the solo violinist — two very different musical instruments blending to mark the beginning of a new phrase. I, unfortunately, was too loud, too soft, too early, or too late. Help! The dress rehearsal was more difficult than I imagined. When tacet, I lay down on some instrument covers, hoping to get through the afternoon and evening.

Candide and *Chichester Psalms* went especially well that night. When it came time for that much-rehearsed measure in the *Serenade*, I remember holding my hand high in the air to strike the chime. My hand was steady, but I had little to give. I was tired. I prayed a prayer one prays upon recognizing their poverty. "Please God, do for me what I cannot do for myself." Adding, "If people see any good in what I do, let it be You they see." Time seemed to expand. Shushing me, Bernstein gestured for our entrance. I took a breath to prepare. His hand dropped. We played. The moment was perfect. Mr. Goodman met me backstage with hugs and praise. I was blessed.

Left to my own devices, there was not even the illusion of having anything to draw on. I asked for help. It came. A power much greater than myself took over and allowed me to experience the fullness of human potential.

From then on, going to Carnegie was like going to church or temple. This great hall is one of those sacred spaces where you can expect to encounter the Holy. It's a fine place to pray.

A Red Rose over My Chest

JOSEPH "GO" MAHAN

A cabaret performer offers a novel view
of the prayerful life.

I WAS BAPTIZED in the Catholic Church as Joseph An-
drew Mahan. Years later upon the commencement of
my career as a cabaret performer in New York City, I rechris-
tened myself as Go Mahan — a childhood nickname that
I thought would complement my quasi-drag androgynous
performing persona. While it has never been my attempt to
impersonate women, I found it artistically liberating to perform as a gender-free entity. The entire performing canon
would be mine regardless of any specific intention of gender
given by the author of its creation.

Growing up Catholic, I attended Catholic school for
twelve years and was taught by nuns. As a boy soprano,
I sang in the church choir not only because I loved to sing,
but because I was allowed to wear a long, black, floorlength
"gown." I was enthralled and mesmerized by the ceremony

of the Catholic mass. The music, the candles, the incense, the stained-glass windows, the stage (altar), the audience (congregation), the costumes (robes), etc. The conjuring and calling of a Higher Power, or, "prayer," if you will, never failed to fill me with awe, and to inspire. For a spell of my early adulthood I attended mass on an almost daily basis. I would pray, and fast, "religiously."

The direct parallels and the inspiration of the Catholic Church on my own personal performing style are undeniable. The intense, several-hours-long process which I undergo in readying myself for the stage allows me the opportunity to concentrate, focus, collect, and calm myself, to slow down, to "go deeper," to tap into a place of "quiet," to clear my head and my Heart. To prepare to "open and connect" to, and from, a Spiritual center. And to hopefully, by virtue of my own open Heart, touch another, via the instrument of song.

I shave my head. I shave my face. I wash myself clean. I apply white makeup. I circle my eyes with black, fine, perfectly drawn lines. I hold my breath and, with exceeding attention and care, outline my lips, then paint them in. I color each individual eyelash. I apply silver glitter to the glistening dome of my bald head. I paint my nails to match the color of my Heart. All is set, and finished, and softened with white matte translucent powder. I slip into a long, black, floor-length gown. I pin a red rose over my chest or dangle a rhinestone cross from around my neck. The three-hour ritual which occurs before every performance allows me silence, calm, clarity, connection, and hopefully the courage to sing the Truth.

In October 2001, I performed my show "At the Altar of My Joy and Sorrow," in the wake of a world weeping. Crumbled Towers, shattered Hearts, and me, with my throat full of tears, trying in some small way to heal a Heart, and mend a City.

Prison Prayers

MARK PEAVEY AND LYNNE DUNNINGTON PEAVEY

A jailed husband and his wife pray.

I AM WRITING THIS from prison. I also am writing it from the heart, just like you should do when you pray.

When I first started getting into trouble, I didn't pray. I didn't believe God would listen to me, but I was wrong. It had been about eighteen years since I had prayed for anything. When I was arrested (for aggravated assault on a peace officer and driving under the influence), I asked God for forgiveness. Would I even get a response since I didn't believe for all those years? I knew in my heart that I was a good person, but I was confused about my life.

In jail, I started praying that I would stop drinking for good, and I can say that I do not have the desire to drink anymore. I have been tempted many times here in prison, but I have always walked away.

I have prayed for many things while I have been locked up. I know for certain God is in my life now. I am going to take one day at a time, get better, and move on. Let God take over and guide me down the right path. Everything is God's will, and if you have faith and pray from your heart, he will deliver what you need. It might not be what you want, but it will be what He wants, I am sure of it.

I have prayed for my family to be there when I get out. I had no idea how my wife and kids would make ends meet without my income, but every single need my family has had has been fulfilled. My wife has stayed with me through this whole ordeal. I was sure she would leave me for good. She had already left me once, and this time it was worse. I have prayed about this many times. Now, my wife and I are more in love than I ever thought possible.

This bad thing that has happened to me was a blessing in disguise. I didn't even have a high school education, but I studied in prison and obtained my GED. My wife and I have written a book together and shared our story with other families and inmates. I have learned to be patient and praise God for a loving wife and wonderful family. Prayer has helped me to understand my problems. There are no problems too big for God.

This experience has been life-altering for me. I have found God and am getting to know him better each day. If it wasn't for prison, I would've never learned to pray. My wife would have left me. I pray that my wife and kids will forgive me. I know God has!

Just recently, my grandmother died. I couldn't go to the funeral. I was very upset. My wife asked me to write a letter to my grandma days before she died. I thought, "Why bother?" She was on her deathbed and couldn't understand anyone; she was incoherent. I wrote the letter anyway, and prayed about it, that she could just hear the letter before she died. My father read it to her. They told me she was awake and listening as my dad read it. They thought she might have understood why I wasn't there. She was going to a better place, and I felt like I was there in spirit to say good-bye. I prayed for something I had no control over, but I felt like God let her hang around long enough to hear my letter. I have a sense of closure. Now I can grieve over her and move on, just like she would've wanted. God answered my prayer. Otherwise, I couldn't forgive myself for being in prison when she died. The power of prayer is awesome. It works for me. I look forward to the future with prayer and my newfound life.

— Mark Peavey
In memory of Marion Peavey (1918–2004)

When you love who has been sent to prison, you must make a choice: either you stay and support them the best way you can, or you walk away and live your life as though they no longer exist. When my husband was arrested, I was so angry I didn't want to see him or speak to him. I would have asked him for a divorce right then. I would have yelled at him, called him names, and probably slapped him, my anger was so intense. Lucky for me, we weren't allowed to speak for a week. Lucky for me, I had time to stop and breathe, to sit and be quiet and ask God, "What should I do?" Lucky for me, He answered "wait." Lucky for me, there's no such thing as luck, but God was answering Mark's prayers that I wouldn't leave.

The first time I saw Mark after his arrest, I was still angry with him, but it was obvious that God was doing a good work in him. He was at peace. He asked forgiveness. He asked for prayer. He was becoming the man of faith that I had prayed for many years earlier. I chose to wait and see what God would do, and discovered that God could pour out his blessings even while Mark was in prison. As I began counting blessings, there were soon enough to fill a book: a renewed commitment to our marriage, shared dreams for the future, better appreciation of family, and a thankful heart.

Not that life has been easy. Our income was cut in half overnight, and there was no hope that Mark would be able to provide financially in the near future. There were legal fees, and I had to take a hard look at the budget to trim costs. Suddenly I was a single parent, managing the house and kids, but I wasn't single and had to do errands for Mark, too. My to-do list got longer and longer. Besides the everyday chores, I was consulting lawyers and writing letters to the parole board. I needed help but felt ashamed and couldn't tell casual acquaintances about my situation. I became more and more frustrated with the legal system. Mark was often restless, worried, and impatient. It was a struggle to maintain a positive attitude. But as we wrote letters and shared our hopes, reminding each other of favorite scriptures and praying together during visitation and phone calls, our relationship grew stronger. Prayer kept our focus on God and each other, enabling us to see the many blessings surrounding us.

Although prayer has sustained us through the past few years, there was a time when we needed more. When Mark's trial was approaching, I felt overwhelmed by anxiety. It was worse for Mark. Our prayers didn't seem to be "enough." My hope was failing. I am not a "prayer warrior," but I know a few: women who glow with the love of Jesus, and can be counted on to faithfully pray every day. I sat down and wrote a letter. Every Christmas, members of my family have a tradition of writing a letter to enclose with their Christmas card, to tell family and friends seldom seen about the year's events. So I wrote a letter explaining the current situation and asking for prayer. The following Sunday, I was in church listening to the music, my thoughts racing, refusing to be quieted. Suddenly, I was at peace, secure in the knowledge that everything would turn out all right. I knew that one of my prayer warriors was lifting me up, right at that very moment, and I was surrounded by love. I felt the connection that all saints have when they pray. Now I often stand in prayer, lifting up Mark. There was a time when he would give any excuse to avoid coming to church with me. Now I know, he would give anything to be in church, standing by my side. That's another blessing. I continue to pray for his peace and safety, knowing that we share a spiritual connection across the miles, and hoping for the day of his homecoming.

—Lynne Dunnington Peavey

Have Mind and Body Healed?

Susan Urbach

A prayer story from the Oklahoma City bombing.

YOU'LL NOT RECOGNIZE my name as a nationally known person. Noteworthy in my own community perhaps, but not in the larger sense. I am, however, part of a notable event, the 1995 Oklahoma City terrorist bombing. That event ushered in the possibility that mass terrorism could happen even here, and even from one of our own. On that morning there was no portent in the sky to say that something would be different. I, and thousands like me, just went to work that morning. In literal seconds, life irrevocably changed for so many. On that morning, you either lived or died. One hundred sixty-eight dead, eighty-three hospitalized, five hundred plus injuries treated and released, and no one found alive after early afternoon of that day. I am one of the eighty-three.

Have mind and body healed? The answer is a resounding yes. Did I pray that morning? Indeed. But it was no beautifully crafted, succinctly phrased, Book of Common Prayer–type of prayer. When I was lying in the street in triage, a friend was brought to my side. She had her carotid artery and jugular vein cut, so she was bleeding profusely. I held her unresponsive hand and couldn't pray anything but, "Oh, God!" (She did live.) When I looked from my friend and turned the other way, there was my church, St. Paul's Cathedral, still standing. I didn't see any of the extensive damage that it incurred, but to see that place still there in the middle of hell breaking loose was an incredible anchor for me.

Unless you have been involved in a major community tragedy — mass murder and mass physical destruction, especially one that generates a tremendous amount of publicity and media interest — it's hard to truly understand the overwhelming feelings. From the tragedy, there is so much to deal with. So many unknowns, tremendous grief, and the work of rebuilding lives and also structures. The press of media is double-edged. It lets people know of what's happened and validates the seriousness of it, but it is also overwhelming and can be invasive.

I was hospitalized several days, then taken in by church friends until I was able to return home. Home was not restful either. Chaos reigned. It seemed as if everyone who ever knew me called, visited, or wrote. I'd go out into the backyard and come back to seventeen messages on the answering machine.

I am head of my office, and there were decisions to be made immediately, dealing with traumatized employees, temporary relocations on an unknown timeframe, and so forth. Once the immediate needs were done, I went to St. Gregory's Abbey in Shawnee, Oklahoma, for three days.

I had been there before, and it had been part of my experience from time to time to go to monastic communities for retreat. I knew that I needed to go inside and center with God. I needed to get away from even my family and friends. Physically, I was exhausted. The doctors had told me that your body expends a lot of energy healing, and so I went to sleep much of those three days. When I wasn't sleeping, I participated in the monastic hours of worship and prayer.

In those silences, I knew God was there, and I didn't need to have the words. In the monastic prayers and psalms, there are words of pain and joy that remind me that for thousands and thousands of years, the human condition deals with pain and tragedy as well as delight and joy. In the words of the liturgy, I join those who for hundreds and hundreds of years have said those words.

Then I wrote. I wrote of what happened to me, what happened to those places and people around me that were damaged and destroyed, and what I hoped for the future. It was too overwhelming to tell the same story over and over to everyone who called, so I asked them if I could send that first, and then they could call back and I could go from that point. Those three days grounded me for the journey to come.

The act of writing became my prayer.

I live in a state that is populated by Christians who are predominantly fundamentalist in their theology. I and other survivors go ballistic when we hear loving but trite phrases such as "God won't give you anything you can't handle," or "God chose you to live because he had things for you to do" (as if God didn't have anything for those who died?), and "God wanted more angels in heaven."

I tussled with unanswerable questions in my writing. In the silence of the front porch and with the computer on my lap, I wrestled with evil, free will, grief, mercy, justice, the unfair death, mortality, and other topics. For four years I prayed in writing. One can literally follow the journey of healing in the writing. It has set a pattern for how I pray. I either sit in silence, or walk to let the body go on autopilot. While the mind then goes free, I write.

Writing Icons

SISTER ELLEN FRANCIS, OSH

An icon painter's approach to prayer.

PAINTING AND DRAWING are the most peaceful activities that I've ever experienced. When I was in high school, I would paint when I wanted to retreat and be quiet. In art school, the drawing class felt somewhat like a zendo: in a room full of people, we were all concentrating on the same thing as we worked in silence.

In art school, of course, the quality of the result was of the utmost importance. While I could, at times, go into a quiet and restful place, there was also the pressure to produce beautiful work. The most exquisite artwork is somehow self-aware of the artist's virtuosity. Icons, on the other hand, are called "windows" into holy space and time, and are not primarily works of art. Icons follow the traditional patterns, set by generations of iconographers, and are not signed by the artist. The iconographer strives to be transparent and to be a faithful "writer" of scripture, in images rather than in words.

Before beginning to work in my studio, I light a candle and some incense, and I pray the prayers of an iconographer, which ask for forgiveness of sins and ask for God's help in taking on the awesome responsibility of portraying saints, the Virgin, and Our Lord. I say these prayers before a little icon. It is an icon of Mary of the Sign, and shows Mary with her arms raised in the orans position of prayer. She is both strong and sorrowful. Jesus is in front of her, with his right hand raised in blessing. This icon isn't finished, and I work on it from time to time. As I start to work on it, I think about the joy of Christ's birth and the spear that will pierce Mary's heart. I pray that in the icon, Mary's face will reflect both.

It is something of a miracle that faces emerge at all out of the natural pigments of earth green and yellow ochre and red and white and black. The underpainting is muddy green, and it takes a leap of faith to believe that it will transform into hands, body, feet, and the features of a face. While I mix the pigments and egg yolk, I'm thinking of the techniques: what shades to mix, how liquid they should be. When I first started to write icons, I was mostly absorbed with the techniques, and worried about the quality of the result.

When I start to work on an icon, I always reflect on the life of the saint or words of scripture related to this icon. When I wrote an icon of St. Stephen, I thought about his face that looked like the face of an angel; when I wrote an icon of the baptism of Christ, I thought about the words:

"This is my Son, the Beloved." Each day as I started work on an icon of St. Benedict, I read a chapter of the Rule.

As I begin to write an icon, I can usually forget about technique and just witness as the icon appears. While writing, I am in a place of no words, complete quiet, no mind. It's hard to find words to describe this state, where the mind is truly at rest. The time of writing icons is a holy gift, and I thank God for each day that I can do this. I think it is the closest that I can get to the peace of God in this life.

When I finish an icon, I'm sometimes not completely pleased with the finished result, and it is always a very humbling experience. This judgment of my work is part of returning to an analytical mind after being in the contemplation of writing. I try really hard not to be disappointed, but to let the icon go as it is and as a gift of the heart.

Once a week, I go to my teacher's studio on Staten Island. On the subway, I bump elbows with men and women who are dressed for Wall Street, while I'm dressed for the studio, in jeans and sneakers. They are scrubbed and full of purpose. I am scruffy, and I pass by the Wall Street stop. I won't be getting off the subway, as I did for a while, to minister at Ground Zero. I won't even be feeding the hungry, comforting the bereaved, or working for social justice and peace among nations. For this day, I'll put aside active ministry and service, and do work of little "use." Instead, I'll be creating something that will go out into the world, and God willing, it will serve as a pointer to the Word of God.

The Art
of Being Human
on a Full-Time Basis

ALAN JONES

*Prayer, for the dean of a great cathedral,
is about showing up for one's own life.*

ONE OF THE SADNESSES of my life is that I have gone
through so many days, months, and years only half
awake. I haven't shown up for my own life. Now that I
am in my midsixties I find that I show up more, and I've
come to realize that prayer for me is a matter of showing
up, being truly present. I still do many of the things I've
done for years. I try to say the daily office (that's one of
the privileges of working with a small "college" of wonderful colleagues — we say Morning Prayer together at Grace
Cathedral). I attend and celebrate the Eucharist regularly.
In fact, it is the one thing that has sustained me through
the years. I also love the aid I receive from little Catholic practices like saying the rosary, lighting a candle before

179

the Icon of the Madonna and Child (I do that on a regular basis), and praying for the protection of the angels. No doubt some people would find such practices odd or cute. But they would be wrong. These practices of mine are a way of affirming that everything is connected and every creature is held in being by a loving hand.

One of the things besides getting older that helps me wake up and be present is my having prostate cancer. It was diagnosed about ten years ago, and I have had no surgery or radiation or any other kind of intervention. There's nothing like learning you have cancer to get your attention! I became part of a scientific study to see if lifestyle change (diet, exercise, stress reduction, and the like) could stabilize or even reverse prostate cancer. As a result I added daily meditation and yoga to the peculiar Anglican mix of my prayer life and, in consultation with a Chinese physician specializing in complementary medicine, my prayers have been given new focus. How? First by affirming that consciousness/spirit is present everywhere, right down to the molecular level. It is a radical affirmation of the Incarnation. Spirit enlivens matter. The Chinese doctor taught me three ingredients to my prayers for my health. First to say, "I love you!" Second to ask for healing. And third to say "Thank you!" Simple. But not simpleminded.

So, my prayer life, as a result, is really a matter of showing up at my own life, which means learning to be grateful for every moment and to be *present* to the One who is always and everywhere present to me, to the world. That's why everything that happens to me can be turned into prayer — the prayer of gratitude. I think what a poem, a piece of music, let alone another human being, does to me. I think how ordinary experiences shape my sense of the future. Is the world a hospitable place or not? The critic George Steiner writes, "To be 'indwelt' by music, art, literature, to be made responsible, answerable to such habitation as a host is to a guest — perhaps unknown and unexpected — at evening, is to experience *the commonplace mystery of a real presence.*"[1] There you have my spirituality in a nut-shell — the grateful celebration of Real Presence. What a privilege — to make present, for an instant, something real — in the face of death. I think of the vitality and gen-erosity of spirit of a great soul like Isabel Allende. About her daughter Paula's dying she wrote, "I finally understood what life is about; it's about losing everything. Losing the baby who becomes a child, losing the child who becomes an adult, like the trees lose their leaves. So every morning we must celebrate what we have."

And there are presences everywhere — things waiting to be seen and touch and experienced — of which the Eu-charist is the supreme sign. The Australian novelist Patrick

---

1. George Steiner, *No Passion Spent* (New Haven, Conn.: Yale University Press, 1996), 35.

White in *Riders in the Chariot* has a character ask the question, "Do you see everything at once? My own house is full of things waiting to be seen. Even quite common objects are shown to us when it is time for them to be." I love the story of the woman who said to the painter, Turner, "I don't see clouds and water like that." "Don't you wish you could, Madam?" he replied.

Finally, prayer for me is practicing the art of being human. It is not so much a matter of pious practices or devotional methods. Prayer is concerned with issues of humanization and dehumanization. Will, the "adult" hero in Nick Hornby's novel *About a Boy* (which was made into an excellent movie), finally grows up when he realizes that he can't opt out of being alive and being wrapped up in the lives of others. "Will couldn't recall ever having been caught up in this sort of messy, sprawling, chaotic web before; it was almost as if he had been given a glimpse of what it was like to be human. It wasn't too bad, really; he wouldn't even mind being human on a full-time basis."[2] The spiritual quest might be defined as our seeking ways to be human on a full-time basis. In fact, this, for me, is what it means to be a Christian. It means being in a never-ending process of learning. This learning involves being pregnant with possibility and suffering the ups and downs of the human

---

2. Nick Hornby, *About a Boy* (New York: Riverhead/Penguin Putnam, 1998), 292.

adventure. It involves our finding ways to live together in community. So, prayer is about being a human being on a full-time basis.

When I was young I was given four pieces of advice: focus on the human being as the place where God chooses to dwell; practice the art of self-simplification; refuse to live in illusion; and be gentle with yourself. It's a long journey. We get lost. We need help. We have to learn to live with uncertainty, doubt, and mystery. But we're in this together — those who pray and those who think they don't.

Why Aren't I My Father's Son?

FRANK DEFORD

*A National Public Radio commentator
and sportswriter's prayer life.*

ONE OF THE distinct memories I retain of my father is that every night just before he went to sleep, he would get down by the side of his bed and kneel, clasping his hands above the bedcovers, closing his eyes in prayer. Even when I was a child and he was a grown man...even when he was an old man in his seventies, he looked like a little boy, there praying in that classic form.

I adored my father. He was an impeccable gentleman, decent to a fault, of fine taste and good humor, and I dearly hope that just some of his sterling character rubbed off on me. Still, as much as we truly admired and loved one another, we didn't have a whole lot in common. I didn't take on his habits. I didn't ever start to garden or raise chickens or wear boutonnieres the way Daddy did. And, as you might have guessed by now, I never took to kneeling by the side of my bed every night and saying my prayers before the sandman carried me off.

So, I have no excuses that I don't pray nearly as much as I should — or as I wish that I should. When I do pray, I like it a great deal. It gives me comfort and reassures me, and (I believe) it draws me closer to God.

So why aren't I my father's son? Why don't I pray as much as I should? I think it's because the way so many people pray strikes me as (what I think is) out of line. Benign, unintentional, but just not quite right. Maybe I first started noticing this in my prime vocation, as a sportswriter. Entirely too many athletes pray for victory. (Even if they just say they're praying that no one gets hurt or to have a good game, or some such thing — trust me, between the lines it's: *and, oh by the way, Lord, help us guys be the ones who win*). Not enough athletes (or other people) remember what Joe Louis, who was not a theologian, said during World War II. He said America would win *not* because "God is on our side," but because "we are on God's side." Not enough of us get that right-side-up, the way the old, unlettered champ did. As touched as I am when someone is saved from some horrible tragedy, I am, still, put off when the person rescued says something to the effect about how God was with them. Excuse me: God *chose not* to be with the other poor devils who didn't get rescued? Maybe I've gotten myself all too twisted up in sacramental minutiae, like the Pharisees or the Sadducees or whoever the ones were who couldn't see the forest for the trees. It's even reached a point where I become a little uneasy hearing "God Bless America" because I get the uncomfortable feeling that we're asking God to concentrate on blessing us Americans, who have so much, when He should be looking out for Haiti and the Sudan instead. If God is the great and good God I believe He is, and yet He allows us free will, I find myself limited in how I might pray to Him, especially appeal to Him. Well, I do thank God a lot, because I know I'm very blessed — whether or not God had anything to do with the largesse granted me in this world I was born into.

On the other hand, I have, I believe, found something of a way around my inability to pray as much as I should to the Lord God. My daughter, Alexandra, died of cystic fibrosis when she was eight. I go out to her grave and sit there and more or less chat with her. I have no trouble asking her to be something of a guardian angel — or perhaps, tacitly, some sort of intermediary to God. So I shoot the breeze with Alex very comfortably, and then go on my way. I think this is a form of prayer, my prayer. I imagine this all sounds primitive and terribly superstitious. I wish, like Daddy, that I could just kneel down by the bed and pray straight-up to God every night, but I've complicated things too much, so I just try and do the best I can.

Mother Broke Her Hip

MALCOLM BOYD

A son learns humble prayer lessons
from tending to an elderly, incapacitated parent.

*B*EATRICE, MY MOTHER, was remarkable through her eighties and into her nineties. She lived in her own home, took care of her dogs, and — even after she had to give up driving a car — managed very well with the help of friends and neighbors.

I was visiting her the day the accident happened. I saw her fall. I think that I knew instinctively something very, very serious had occurred — yet, at the same time, I didn't really grasp it. I ran to her, helped her to stand up, and got her seated in a chair. She didn't indicate she was in pain. We chatted as if nothing was unusual about the situation. Then, suddenly, she said, "I think I broke my hip." I replied that I'd better call 911 and have an ambulance come.

Mother said, quietly, "Let's just sit here for a while." But I knew we couldn't. I placed the call, an ambulance arrived. Now she was in great pain. The attendants placed her body on a gurney, and they drove off. I followed in my car. At the hospital her surgery was scheduled in a few hours. It was successful, but Beatrice was never to see her home again. After a few days in the hospital, she was sent to another one for a month of treatment, including exercise. Then, I was informed, she would have to be placed in a nursing home — really more of a convalescent hospital.

All this was on-the-job training for me. I knew nothing of the practicalities of such an institution. I'd visited people in nursing homes, yes, but behind-the-scenes stuff was a mystery to me. I caught on fast because I had to make decisions now. I decided on one nursing home which, mercifully, turned out to be an excellent choice.

So began the next four and a half years, which culminated in Mother's death just ten days before her ninety-ninth birthday.

The beginning was not auspicious. Beatrice reacted against this new experience in her life with its unfamiliarity, harshness, and absence of much personal freedom. She occupied a room with two other older women. Because of her fear and stress, it was necessary to restrain her body both in bed and a wheelchair in order to keep her from falling down. Clearly, she didn't understand what was happening to her.

Then she moved resolutely toward an attitude of acceptance. Always her faith had been a bulwark. Now it became the central great force of her life.

I was deeply affected by this presence, this example. I saw depths of courage in it, levels of patience and an enduring hope that transcended present circumstances. Beatrice remained grace-filled, interiorly calm and peaceful, clearly at peace with the world. She chose to smile instead of frown, seemingly enjoy her endlessly reflective moments instead of rail against them in a frustrated or even bitter way.

We had never been demonstratively physical together. However, now I held her close at the end of each time I visited. And held on. Also we always concluded a visit of mine by saying together the Lord's Prayer (in the traditional old form using the word "trespasses"). Doing this over a period of months and years gradually changed many of my feelings concerning this signature prayer. I became more intimate with it and discerned meanings that were fresh, challenging, immediate.

The point is: I had to enter into the experience of the nursing home, too. It became a central locus of my spiritual life. I couldn't enter and depart with alacrity or noninvolvement. I had to acknowledge deep roots of my own in that place. I got to know people working there, other patients (and their families and friends), the smell and feel of the place, moods, sadnesses, and tiny points of joy. So my prayer life changed. It inescapably had to contain the nursing home and all the things going on there. I had to give up any sense of control, and surrender to the realities of the situation. I couldn't dictate anything; I could only see, feel — and pray.

Beatrice's death was an exemplary one. She had been seemingly unconscious, but now she opened her eyes, looked directly into mine, grasped my hand firmly — very, very firmly — and let go. I think I know exactly where she was going, up through a dark corridor toward the light.

Beatrice's years in the nursing home taught me more about prayer than Sunday school or seminary ever did, and I remain eternally grateful.

The Jung Group in a Synagogue

Nan C. Gold

*A psychotherapist reaches for help
beyond psychotherapy. . . .*

*I*T WAS 4:00 a.m., and I was lying in bed frozen with fear. My husband was having great difficulty breathing. For months we had been seeing doctors, trying to figure out why he was so tired and easily winded. Two months earlier — upon the suggestion of the cardiologist — he had had a pacemaker put in. Pain in his shoulder at the site of the implant led us to believe that a nerve had been injured, but just a few days before the surgeon had ruled that out.

His breathing became more and more troubled as I lay there immobilized beside him that night. I knew any move to get help would further upset him. I wanted him to remain calm. Finally I decided that the only hope of getting him to a doctor would be to somehow call 911 without him knowing I was doing so. I went downstairs "for a drink of water" and made the call. "No sirens please," I requested.

That night and the weeks that followed marked a turning point in my prayer life.... First things first. Let me begin by telling you something about me and my prayer life until that point.

I am a fifty-seven-year-old Jewish woman who was raised in a Reform Jewish home in Texas. I have been married for twenty-two years to a man who is several years my senior and who was raised in an Orthodox Jewish environment. We attend a Modern Orthodox temple on a regular basis and are involved in its activities. My husband is a vice president of the temple.

Being a psychotherapist, I am familiar with the pathos, intricacies, stress, and variable conditions of life. Sometimes psychotherapy alone is not enough.

My exposure to a new meaning of prayer came from two very different places. The first was a group of psychotherapists that I have belonged to for twenty years. The second was my synagogue. The Jung Group is a group of seven women who have been meeting for twenty years. In this safe and loving community I have been privileged to observe people close to me who have been through early childhood traumas, health crises, and social injustices far worse than I have experienced. As a therapist I know that such experiences can leave one feeling angry, depressed, anxious, and powerless. Yet due to the masterful guidance of the group leader, these amazing people have found a way to thrive and, in fact, transform those experiences into a way of being that enables them to reach out in loving service to others.

I consider this group leader to be my spiritual mentor. She leads most strongly by example and is an inspiration to all who know her. I have watched her deal with her own pain and suffering in a way that goes beyond psychotherapy. She leads her life in constant communication with God without cutting off, no matter what. Her relationship with God is hands-on. She can be angry at God, joyful, grateful. She can question, petition. No matter what, she lives consciously in God's presence, and this presence is a constant source of strength for her. Based on her faith (not Jewish) she views things with a bigger picture in mind and does not lose herself in herself. Her sensitivity and generosity have benefited many. She has shared some of her thinking as well as her faith with me and others in the group. This has provided me with the possibility of a new way to be with God.

My husband came so very close to dying. It was only through a series of miracles that he was saved. Miracles like a doctor stopping by and deciding to do an angiogram immediately rather than waiting until it was scheduled — an on-call doctor arriving who provided an option that nobody else had thought of — the extraordinary clarity and strength of mind given to my husband to enable him to decide what to do when even tremendously skilled surgeons were hesitant to proceed.

When there were no good options I prayed for help and it came. I learned that some prayers are answered in ways not expected. During this whole process there were prayers of our temple, as well as prayers by others, many of whom did not know my husband or me. I have never experienced such love. I learned that a community of pray-ers does make a difference.

This series of miracles in which prayers were answered has made a profound shift within me and deepened the way in which I pray. One change is that in my most vulnerable state I discovered that I was not alone. The communication with God was constant, and I was guided. I do believe that God does talk to me and others by planting ideas in our hearts and our heads. I now know that what I communicate to God through prayer and action does have impact, even if the prayers are not always answered as I think I would like. This realization has changed the quality of my prayer life. I spend more time praying, both alone and as part of a congregation. In a typical day I will say a prayer of gratitude when I wake up, thanking God for Creation, good health, my husband, family, and friends. I will pray for strength to do what is put before me and to be of service. As I read the paper or listen to the news I will pray for those in need of healing, for peace, and for the ability to do something that promotes it. From time to time I will say prayers in honor of my parents and sister, who are deceased. At night, before I go to bed I will thank God for the day and the good things that have happened during the day. I pray that God will bless and protect loved ones and bring healing to those who suffer. During the day I might have a conversation with God for whatever reason. As I have benefited from the prayers of others and seen it help, I want to give back by being more mindful of the needs of others.

Writer's Block or Artist's Block

Steve Ross

A professional illustrator draws the line on prayer.

$\mathscr{A}$ T ONE END of my studio, I'm staring at a very white, blank sheet of drawing paper. In another corner is a computer monitor with a very blank word processing document staring coldly back at me. My Hobson's choice: writer's block or artist's block. Take your pick.

I was asked to write about prayer. The deadline has now passed. I'm also weighted down under a feverishly self-imposed deadline on a graphic novel about, of all things, the Gospel according to Mark. On this cold December morning, it seems like I say yes to way too much. At some point I begin to regret all those "yeses."

The creative process has been written about by more talented writers than myself. But my own process is marked by prayer. No, I don't get down on my knees in front of my easel and pray for guidance. Well, not exactly. But I often find myself consciously placing myself in the hands of something more gracious and less stingy than myself.

What does that prayer look like? It starts with a breath, indistinguishable from a sigh. I put my pencil down. The morning isn't going well.

Some days, I look at my work and laugh, the way I laugh when my own children surprise and delight me with their audacity and fearlessness. Today isn't one of those days.

There is a great temptation to pick up the eraser and scrub everything out. I look at my creation, stunted and halfhearted. I close my eyes and wonder where I went wrong. Why does everything I draw today seem like crap?

And that's when I stumble through the open door. The dialogue starts.

"I never said it would come easily every time."

"But why today, God? Why can't it be just a little bit easier? I've labored for hours this morning and nothing works."

"Just draw a line."

"What?"

"You heard me. Just put a mark on paper. That's all I ask."

I put a squiggle on the paper. Feeling particularly willful, I sketch an insipid smiley face.

"See, that's the best I can do. I'm all dried out." I expect a reprimand, God commanding me to suck it up and quit whining.

"Draw another line," is all the voice says.

I draw another line. I can't resist making this one a little more descriptive. It's a squiggle that might resemble a man leaning over. Hmm, is he feeding a dog? I draw a little dog.

"But this has nothing to do with my project. My deadline has come and gone. Am I just going to doodle all day?"

"Perhaps. Would that be so bad?"

It would be nice at this point to say that I receive a brilliant flash of inspiration. The scales fall from my eyes, and I see how the drawing of the little man feeding the dog fits perfectly into the story. "But of course," I smile to myself. "It's perfect!" I'm humbly grateful before my God. My "prayer" has been answered. I sketch away, happily redeemed by the power of God, who has cleverly tricked me out of my artist's block. Hallelujah!

The fact is that the man and his dog do not belong in the story. Nor does the next drawing of a school bus filled with tentacled squid children. Or the sketch of a juggling harlequin. Or any of the next twenty-five, fifty, or one hundred drawings and sketches and dead ends and blind alleys that take up the rest of the day.

But the next morning, as I stare at the ugly blank sheet, weighed down by the remembrance of all the false starts from the previous day, I hear the voice again.

"Just draw me a line. That's all."

I draw a line.

This scenario has repeated itself often enough over the years to have become a familiar reality for me, as familiar as any prayer I have said thousands of times in church. And it ends the same way, with sometimes just a tenuous thread to get me to the next stumbling block.

But that's okay. My prayer as an artist has never been to be given the answer. No, my prayer at the drawing table is that I never stop looking.

A Clearer Picture

Jeff Allin

For this theater and television actor, it's all prayer.

NOT HAVING HAD much religious training as a boy, I never had a very large space in my life for the idea of prayer. I suppose I attempted to "talk to God" when I needed or wanted something badly enough, in spite of the embarrassment I inevitably felt. I do remember, though, that my dad seemed to have a special affinity for the great, open, outdoor vistas of the Arizona desert in which we lived. At some point in my youth it became clear to me that, whether he was on horseback, on foot, or traveling by car, those open, uncluttered spaces gave my father a sense of where he fit. A visceral knowing, it must have been his own way of communing with something greater than himself.

I bring it up because, as a fifty-two-year-old man who has spent the last twenty-some years as an actor in the television and theater world, I now have a much clearer picture of what constitutes prayer for me.

Whether alone in my morning meditation, in communion with some part of myself; on a yoga mat in class, going on thirty years now, in silent communion as we stretch and unfold; or on a stage, opening and sharing with hundreds of strangers in a search for some larger understanding, it's all prayer to me. Sitting beside my twelve-year-old daughter as she thrills to the dance troupe in front of us, listening to my son's jokes and stories at the dinner table, celebrating twenty years of marriage with my wife, it's all prayer to me.

I still talk to God, although I don't always call Her that. I'm not embarrassed.

Thank You

JANE TULLY

A mother's prayer of thanksgiving for her gay son.

THANK YOU, God, for my beautiful gay son.

Thank you for the day he was born, when his warm, wet little body first lay on my breast.

Thank you for the memory of his curly two-year-old head under my chin as we read *Oh, What a Busy Day!* on the couch.

Thank you for his little-boy laugh and the time we spent all afternoon at the Washington Monument when the cherry trees were blooming.

Thank you for the kite flying and our Sheltie chasing us across the park.

Thank you for the skating and the hot chocolate on Saturdays.

Thank you for the bright pink Queer Dance invitation he handed me when he said, "Mom, I have something to tell you."

Thank you for Mozart's *Don Giovanni*, which he played at full blast every afternoon in his seventeenth year.

Thank you for his big warm heart and goofy sense of humor.

Thank you for his health.

Thank you for his love of reading and gift for writing.

Thank you for his friends, his job, and his independence.

Thank you that he has his own place and I no longer have to do his laundry or clean up his room.

Thank you for the stories he tells me about all his friends.

Thank you for the time he took me to see his favorite drag queen perform, dressed like a Christmas tree.

Thank you for his college degree, all paid for.

Thank you for the rings in his ears and chin, the amazing star tattoos on his elbows, and a thousand other ways he makes me laugh.

Thank you for his sweet boyfriend.

Thank you for bringing them both home for Thanksgiving and letting me see them hugging and holding hands, just like all the rest of us.

Thank you for showing me my beautiful gay son in love.

Thank you for the incredible gift of my beautiful son.

Following the Breadcrumbs

Cynthia Rush

*A professional photographer takes photographs
of remnants of meals — and discovers that our times
of fellowship together are emblems of prayers prayed.*

I PICKED UP a camera thirty years ago and took a photo
that would become a prayer I'm still praying. At the
time, it was one of many photos, taken casually on an island
vacation. It would never have occurred to me that it could
be a prayer.

The photo was a close-up of the remains of a breakfast
eaten out of doors. I remember two white plates; traces of
egg yolk, a sand dollar with a delicate hollow; two glass
mugs holding shallow pools of coffee; the sliced pink oval
of a papaya, its center brimming with plump, dark seeds.
All of these shimmered on a round stone tabletop in early
morning tropical light.

When I got back to my everyday existence as an artist
living in Soho, I looked through my stack of vacation photos. That one gave me pause. I set it aside on my drafting

table and glanced at it from time to time. Like the grain of sand that sticks in an oyster, the image of what was left after the meal started working on me.

Why did it intrigue me that there were no people? Their absence made me look at the table itself. As if deciphering a tarot card or shards from an archeological dig, I had to read the food remaining on the plates and the objects used during the meal as clues to the humanity of the two who had shared it. I saw the narrow path of a fork where it had scraped a pale yellow streak through egg yolk; the tilt of a papaya slice left half-eaten, the lacy pattern of milk froth inside the glass of one mug, the rumpled fold of a cloth napkin tossed aside.

I looked again, and again. Shapes emerged in repetition. Rims of the two mugs echoed the roundness of the plates. The round stone tabletop encircled the roundness of spoons, papaya seeds, and slivers of cooked egg whites. The chalky round presence of the sand dollar was at the table's center.

What would I come up with, I wondered, if I kept making photographs after meals, after the diners had left the table? That was where my prayer began, in that interval of mystery any artist will recognize. The writer William Stafford calls it "that precious little area of confusion when I do not know what I am going to say and then I find out what I am going to say. That precious interval I am unable to bridge by skill."

I started following the breadcrumbs of my hunch. I began taking "After Meals" photographs — anywhere — in my studio, at a friend's, in a restaurant, after a hot dog eaten on a park bench or after eating off the fold-out tray in an airplane. I avoided using any flash on the camera, even to photograph a meal by candlelight. I made a conscious effort not to think about my angle of vision or a particular vantage point when I got up from the meal to shoot. I wanted to capture the immediacy of consummation when the experience ran its course to become a whole.

I took hundreds of photographs of my daily meals in the first few months. I just kept going and tried not to judge until I could see if they held up over time. I tried to be nonchalant when I was eating with others, rather than alone. I'd casually remove my camera from my shoulder bag as the meal drew to a close, and shoot. I got used to looks of bewilderment. Though I thought I might be wasting my time, I was riding on a sense of wonder, and I was held in the throes of what photographer Cartier-Bresson calls "trying to reach eternity through the moment."

I spun out a longer and longer visual thread, and my photographs gained in their growing relationship to one another. I began to see that they were illuminating the act of savoring. We often miss out on the moment after our meals, the moment of completion, because we rush to clean up, to get on with life, to cross the next thing off endless to-do lists.

I chose the best of the photos I'd taken to make up the first "After Meals" series. Two years later, the rhythm of my life seen in the microcosm of the meal hung on the walls of the Leo Castelli Gallery in New York. Thirty years and three lives later, I've created many other bodies of work, but I keep adding to my "After Meals" photographs. Now I'm weaving one hundred of the photos into a book with accompanying narrative.

I'm still not sure where this is headed or why I keep on, but I do know that each photograph is a prayer of connection, a prayer of patience and being present, a prayer of longing for intimacy with a harmony deep in the nature of things, a prayer of thanksgiving for consummation and the possibility of beginning anew in the mystery of the ordinary.

Three Prayers from a Young Adult Weekend

SPENCER SMILANICK, TINIA ORDUÑA,
AND HOLLY MARTIN

I.

Hi God

Thanks for having me

Lord, you are my #1. All I have is Yours. I just wish You'd speak up sometimes. I want to have faith in You in all things, but I don't know where my responsibility starts and stops. What should I do? At what point am I working so hard that I'm not trusting You?

I WANT A JOB. I try to trust you more than money, Lord, but I need money. I do. You have shown me I don't need to fear. But my funds are running short. I'm running out of time. I'm going to work as hard as I can, and I trust that You will work with me. I'm not afraid yet. . . .

Or am I?

I'm afraid of people not respecting me. I've worked so hard to show the world that I'm strong. Have I not been humble? I don't want those around me to look at me and say "Ah, he's just a screwed-up kid. He isn't an Adult. He isn't reliable. He isn't strong."

I'm going to try harder. I will. You'll see. I hope to see You on the road. I'll be the one trying to be like You (the guy next to the guy doing a good job).

What next?
What next Lord?
How long will You test me?
I'm scared and lost and lonely.
Please hold me Lord. I'll be okay, but I hate not knowing when.
I still haven't been loving my neighbor. Sorry, I suck. You know.

I don't want a handout. I'm willing to work for what I want. I just can't get a break right now.
I don't want another poor Christmas.
I want to have success.
Help me please.

— *Spencer Smilanick*

II.

Spirit of gentleness, blow through the wilderness, wind, wind on the sea. Funny how I have to look to nature and dirt, trees, grass, the cold air to find you.

Why do you escape me so? Do you really love me? My prayer is for peace. What does that mean? It means, let me break it down —

I want to feel deep in my core that I am loved by you. To know I am a child of God. That the pain and anguish and injustice I feel inside is felt by you.

Remove my heavy and I mean heavy yoke and set me free.

Enliven, breathe into, work your thing in me so that I am truly alive again, walking day to day not in mundane existence but in passionate, soaring, fiery life. The life I believe you intended for me.

I know I'm getting closer. I just still don't know what that trust looks like. I get embarrassed and angry at you for my tears, but you gave me a pretty strong heart. A heart that burns with passion. Yeah I'm selfish. I know I shouldn't be but I am.

God, will you hear me when I cry — yes — but perhaps even more important to me is will you respond?

So much I don't get. (Typical.) I want the answers yesterday — but I'm probably not ready for them. Will I ever be a star? Will I ever act again? Will I ever have a vacation?

Will I ever be somebody? A Mother Teresa, a Gandhi, Martin Luther King Jr., Maya Angelou? Why is it so hard to be an artist? Why is it so hard to be an artist and live in the world? I know I'm definitely not cut out to be an insurance salesperson. One down, only ... to go.

Quiet me God, be my mother, my counselor, my nurturing presence, my healer, my peacemaker.... Here.... These are all my burdens rushing like traffic ... getting nowhere in my head. You take 'em. I'm tired, I'm weary, I'm overwhelmed. I'm human.

Rekindle my flame for you. Nourish and feed and grow my spirit again. Make loud your sounds, your presences in my mind and in my ears. Let it flow through me.

Ho ho ho hosanna. Ha ha ha le luia. He saved me. I am a child of the Lord.

Today trust. Tomorrow joy.

— *Tinia Orduña*

III.

Dear God, when you took my mother I was very hurt. You did not need her up there yet. I don't understand why you took her and I may never understand but you may never give or show me an answer. I know that I need to work this out with you and find some comfort.

One thing I would like from you God is show me where I need to be and how I am going to get there. I need to be more assertive of things that I want. I need to not hold things inside me. I need to tell friends and family how I feel and not hurt them in the process. Please help or show me how.

God, I would like you to show me a way to tell my father he needs to quit smoking. I need you to show me. I need to not try to compare myself with others. I know I am not them and I should be my own self. God I wish that you would guide my sister.

I want to experience you as I know others around me have. I am amazed at how you choose your disciples and how you have them share their experiences with me and everyone in the world.

God, I know I am not perfect and that some people strive for it. Me, I just want to know that every day doing my best is okay. Others may think that is wrong, but I do not and think others look at me and say "Why don't you?" Is it wrong of me to be that way? I know that I have prejudices toward people and that is wrong. Show me a better way and show others as well.

God, I thank you for my parents, friends, family and others that you have brought into my life to try and help me with my struggle. I know I may not have always been listening, but I intend to work on that.

Thank you and God bless.

P.S. If I forgot something, I know you'll show me eventually.

— *Holly Martin*

Prayer in a Hospital

GRETCHEN HAIGHT

A hospital chaplain understands prayer
as an attitude, a way of being.

TUESDAY MORNING 9:25. I'm drinking a cup of coffee before making my rounds as lay hospital chaplain on the eighth floor of the medical center. The phone rings. A nurse from the ICU (Intensive Care Unit) has a request for a chaplain: "The family of James Bennett [not his real name] in 429 could use some help. We're getting ready to remove life support."

"I'll be there in five minutes." I ask if there's anything particular I should know about the patient or his family. "Do you know what religion they are?"

"I don't think they're especially religious. They're in agreement about removing life support. They know he can't get better. They're upset."

"I'll be right there."

In the desk chair I compose myself, feet flat on the floor, back straight in meditative posture. Closing my eyes, I give my body time to relax. I feel a giving way in the base of my spine, my stomach, shoulders, and neck. I think words something like, "Please, God, let me be a channel for your love, peace, and reassurance to this family." I get out my prayer book, marking a couple of prayers that might be appropriate if the family would like formal prayer. For some, such language helps elevate the moment into more sacred dimensions than what fits their own words. But for others, formal prayers seem disconnected from themselves, not their own. Worse, they can arouse associations with church or religion that are negative. So they wish to express their grief and hope in their own words and thoughts.

In any case, I consider it my task to make sure family and friends have an opportunity to participate in an acknowledgment of the sacredness of this dearly loved person dying. Moving away from them into a different place. None of us knows where the dying person is going. All we can do is be together in the mystery that this loved one has come from God and is returning to God. We can be grateful for a life in all the ways it has affected our own.

I lived more than thirty years (from college age to fifty-two) oblivious to prayer and religion. Perhaps that's why I am sensitive to people like the Bennetts who lack a religious context in which to think about death. They have no ritual meaningful for them to participate in. Yet they love this person who is dying and are sad he is leaving them. Furthermore, even though they know everyone dies, they simply can't believe it. Helplessness and disbelief are not knowing where he is going: these are just a few of the many feelings they might have.

I enter the small room in the ICU, introduce myself to Mr. Bennett's daughter and son. We move outside the room to talk about how they would like to say good-bye to their dad. First I learn their mother is in a nursing home, unaware of what's going on here. They tell me they're not religious, but want to do something. We decide I should start with a general personal prayer, not one from a prayer book. They'll follow with whatever feels important for them to say. They are numb, understandably. And they're grateful for my guidance in making these last moments with their father meaningful.

It is a moment like this, I realize, that defines most clearly for me what prayer really is.

We often say prayer is communication with God, but such a definition suggests talking to God. For me, the words we say — thoughts we think, feelings and imagination we experience in prayer — are all manifestations of how we pray. I believe prayer is an attitude beyond mental images. We sit, or stand, or kneel. We allow ourselves to surrender to the mystery of not knowing instead of trying to comprehend. So, in the mystery of being there with Mr. Bennett, all three of us were in a place of prayer.

Afterward, I sit quietly back in my Spiritual Care Department office. Mr. Bennett died late that night.

Each day I try to begin with prayer and meditation. As my husband and I enjoy spending time together, and our relationship grows and deepens, so I spend time with God for the same reason. No matter whether my time includes verbal prayer, spiritual reading, silent meditation, or just looking out at nearby mountains, it's all communication with God.

My shortcomings (lack of trust, to name one) get in the way, of course, just as they do in all my relationships. I'm no different with God than with anyone else. But I try. In fact, with God I try to not try. Simply surrender to the mystery of God to let the peace that lies deep within that relationship — "the peace that passes all understanding" — have a better chance of becoming the center of my being. This is the place from which I move out into life around me.

How I Prayed on 9/11

Debra A. Wagner

A prayerful first response to a suffering city on 9/11.

$\mathcal{M}$ Y RESPONSE to God's will is jump-started by prayer. Discerning God's will through prayerful reflection leads to action supported by an unflappable resolve. This was especially true for me on September 11, 2001, as I started my day as director of communications for the Seamen's Church Institute of New York & New Jersey, just 850 yards away from the World Trade Center.

Shortly after the first plane struck the North Tower, I watched in horror from my fourth floor window as flames and black smoke poured out from the top floors. Tiny specks of debris began sputtering out of the gaping hole. As the second plane hit the South Tower, a radio on a nearby desk announced word of the unprecedented terror. Looking down on Water Street below, I saw people falling to their knees on the sidewalk, crying, writhing, and calling out names of friends and loved ones.

Some SCI staff members were crying. Others were shaking. My heart started to beat faster as I began to fear more attacks, perhaps a nuclear attack. Many phones on our floor started ringing. Two SCI employees called in from the Brooklyn Battery Tunnel where they were trapped because traffic was halted. One staff member was most likely on her usual PATH train heading into the World Trade Center station.

Where were my husband and two sons?

As a paralyzing dread crept into my psyche, I began to pray, "Our Father who art in heaven." Stopping after the first few words of the Lord's Prayer, I realized that I did not want to be alone with a God who was "in heaven" when it looked like hell around me.

As one of the organizers of our daily prayer service, I asked the Institute's receptionist to announce that chapel would begin in two minutes. The call to chapel service is heard every working day at the Seamen's Church Institute, but this one would surely have special significance. I was drawn to choose the "Prayers for Peace" from our collection of ecumenical prayer services. Every staff member arrived for the short service, where we prayed with fervor for peace in our land. I clenched my teeth when the words called to pray for our enemies. As we began the Lord's Prayer with the wail of sirens from responders in the background, I wondered how God's will could include the death of so many innocent people.

After worship, we went back to answering telephone calls, letting loved ones know that we were alive. My husband managed to call in to let me know that he found our sons and was bringing them to our apartment, which is two miles north of my workplace. Thankfully God's will for them was safety.

The Seamen's Church Institute building still had running water, telephone and Internet service, and air conditioning. I e-mailed reports about what was happening in Lower Manhattan to Episcopal communication colleagues in the New York area.

We kept our doors open to the public as we waited for our executive director to walk in after arriving that morning at a Long Island airport. Feeling safe inside my office, I watched in horror as the first tower collapsed with a loud rumble. The sky grew grayish white as a snowlike dust began to fall. You could see the panic and fear on the faces of people as they tried to run away from the cloud. It was a scene of horror straight from the Old Testament.

How could this really be God's will? I thought as I raced to the lobby. Crowds on the streets surged toward safety across the nearby Brooklyn Bridge or just pushed their way uptown. One woman rushed in sobbing, "My God, they are jumping out the windows." The wife of our cafeteria cook came in covered in dust and ran upstairs to her husband. The second building collapsed, sending a new wave of people covered in dust onto the streets. Some stunned, dazed people wandered into the Institute for a few moments of respite or to use a telephone.

I walked from the lobby to the chapel, repeating the Lord's Prayer, stopping at the words, "Thy Will be done on earth as it is in heaven." How could this be? Your will, and what was Your will for me? God and I were finally alone.

Just then, a brawny young man in his twenties named Guy came through our front door looking for his father, who was on our staff. His body started to tremble as he discovered that the last time we heard from his dad was to let us know that they were in the Brooklyn Battery Tunnel. As I walked over to him, he began to sob for his father and his girlfriend who worked near the World Trade Center. He had just come from a futile attempt to get close to the site. Despite his massive build and obvious strength, he could not penetrate the mobs of fleeing people.

I insisted that we go into the chapel. "No, I've got to find them," he said as I took his trembling hands and guided him to the nearby door. Looking intensely into his eyes and then bowing in prayer, we recited the Lord's Prayer several times. "This really ain't working for me," he said hastily moving out the door and back into the dust-covered streets.

Standing in the lobby was obviously not the right place for me to "do" something. I went back to my office to try to find out more news over the Internet. The phone rang. My husband, safe at home with our two sons, begged me to join them. The television reports they were watching and the F-15 fighters flying overhead added to a growing sense of imminent danger. "Please come home. Your place is with your family," he said. "I need to stay here," I said, unable to articulate any further explanation. We ended the conversation without saying good-bye.

"Thy will be done." A will that included the unimaginable collapse of the Twin Towers bringing death, destruction, and imminent fear into the heart of Americans. A will that filled me with an overwhelming need to remain in a place surrounded by destruction. With a faithful resolve based on a lifetime of prayer, I waited for God to reveal that will. God took mercy on my impatience and only made me wait a few more hours. Then I went into action with courage of my (and God's) conviction.

Postscript: After the arrival of SCI's executive director at noon, the entire staff held a meeting in the chapel. We unanimously decided to begin a twenty-four-hour emergency relief service to first responders using food and drink found in the Institute's second-floor cafeteria. Because most staff members were unable to return to Lower Manhattan after going home that evening, the work of the next three days fell to a few of us who lived nearby. Over those days of intense work we managed to create an oasis of food, safety, and space for prayer for the rescuers and relief workers flooding into the "frozen zone." I was the on-site "coordinator" for those first few days when our neighborhood had no phone service or electricity. I felt woefully unprepared for this task, but with God's graceful response to my prayers, I was able to set up a system that provided a foundation for this expanding relief effort. Supplies and volunteers began to stream into the Institute the next day. On the evening of September 12, more than six hundred weary firefighters, police officers, military, and relief workers ate a hot meal at the Institute. Thirteen days later, this relief effort moved to St. Paul's chapel. By the way, Guy's dad and girlfriend made it home safely.

It Takes a Mountain or
an Ocean

Michael Seiler

*A modern-day Thoreau recommends us
to the spiritual tutelage of mountaintops*

IT WAS LATE AFTERNOON when I set out from Los Angeles, grim and resolute. I had been looking forward to this trip for weeks, and I had planned an early start, but last-minute pressures and unforeseen circumstances delayed my departure until nearly noon. My long-awaited idyll in the mountains began as a traffic-choked trek across the San Fernando Valley. It was not an auspicious start for a four-day retreat in the Yosemite high country.

By early afternoon, I had left the Los Angeles traffic behind and was well on my way, and the cloudless sky and the wide-open highway lifted my spirits. I settled in for the six-hour drive. Breathe deep. Adjust seat back. Air conditioning. Banana. Led Zeppelin CD. The miles rolled away, and by late afternoon I was headed up the long, twisting road into the Sierras. Adjust seat back. Air conditioning off (getting colder outside). U2 CD out, Chopin CD in (getting calmer inside). Just before dusk, I reached the end of the road and parked my car. It was almost sunset — the hour of Vespers.

I'd left Los Angeles in eighty-five-degree weather, but here at seventy-two hundred feet in the Sierra Nevada the temperature was just above freezing. I donned a heavy jacket and gloves, and headed up a trail that climbed through thick pines toward the top of a low ridge. The trail steepened, and in only a few minutes I was out of breath, panting for oxygen in the thin twilight air, but the cold and the altitude seemed to sharpen my senses, the icy spring snow crackling under my footsteps. I crested the top of the ridge, pulse racing, cheeks burning in the chill.

The pines cleared. I took a few more steps, and in an instant the ground seemed to vanish from under my feet. A sudden, stabbing revelation of alpine landscape roared silently up before me, saturating my vision. I was all alone on the South Rim of Yosemite Valley at the hour of Vespers, gazing northeast into the High Sierra, just as the sun set and the alpenglow shone on the snowfields as far as the eye could see. It was a sight of such magnificence and sublimity that I cried out in mingled shock and delight.

The altitude, my racing pulse, the overpowering view, and the nearby brink of the chasm together seemed to force me to the ground. I sat for a moment in awestruck silence, watching the alpenglow deepen from burning orange to violet to velvety indigo. Then I took off my gloves, opened my prayer book, and began Evening Prayer:

> O gracious light,
> pure brightness of the ever-living Father in heaven,
> O Jesus Christ, holy and blessed!
>
> Now as we come to the setting of the sun,
> and our eyes behold the Vesper light,
> we sing your praises, O God: Father, Son, and Holy Spirit.
>
> You are worthy at all times to be praised by happy voices,
> O Son of God, O giver of life,
> and to be glorified through all the worlds.

In that privileged hour of Vespers, I saw, I knew, that the magnificent architecture of the Sierra landscape was the conscious, joyful, radiant handiwork of an unimaginably creative and generous Architect. In that moment of my illumination I knew, as I knew my own soul, that the beauty that surrounded me was only a shadow of the true Beauty who had shaped it. The sunset light on the Sierra crest, the chill air, the stupendous oceans of mountain scenery, all were glorifying God in a silent, enveloping harmony of praise and worship and joy. Prayer seemed to be materializing before my very eyes. How then could I not lend my mind and will to join in the praise and thanksgiving that filled the air, as far as the eye could see?

Your love, O LORD, reaches to the heavens,
and your faithfulness to the clouds.

Your righteousness is like the strong mountains,
your justice like the great deep;
you save both man and beast, O LORD.

How priceless is your love, O God!
Your people take refuge under the shadow of your wings.

They feast upon the abundance of your house;
you give them drink from the river of your delights.

For with you is the well of life,
And in your light we see light.

Psalm 36:5–9

We are needy, hungering souls. We rarely have the presence of mind to feel, let alone the courage to face, our
unfulfilled desire for God, but that desire moves in our
depths whether we acknowledge it or not. And usually, we
don't acknowledge that desire for God. Instead, we narco-
tize it, denounce it, deny it, push it out of our minds, drown
it out in a riot of stimuli and "entertainments." City life,
deadlines, cell phones, twenty-four-hour-a-day sports chan-
nels, and all of the detritus of modern life gradually drain
the desire for God from our souls.

A mountain landscape praises God and invites me to
worship. It presses the praises of God upon me with a kind
of gracious, loving insistence. But a television set praises

not God but deodorants, violence, and the base neuro-
chemical titillations of fear and greed and lust. It presses
upon me not praise, not worship, but marketing strategies. Slowly, imperceptibly, but fatally we turn our wills
and our desires away from the God Whom we truly want,
toward the strange paraphernalia that the oceanic media
in which we swim tells us to want. We suffer from con-
stantly increasing desires for things that satisfy us less and
less. We are overworked, overinformed, overentertained,
overconsuming, and overtired.

We welcome every temptation as a blessing, and resist
every blessing like a temptation. When we master the dubi-
ous art of living comfortably in this bizarre, unnatural state,
we deem ourselves "successful," and then our spiritual fall
from grace is complete.

Within a few days after I returned from my Sierra vacation, my moment of illumination at the hour of Vespers was
all but forgotten. Forgetfulness endarkened its memory, and
its light was obscured in my mind's eye by the routines of
ordinary life, in a kind of slow-motion spiritual eclipse that
lasted not a few astronomical moments, but years. It was
many years since I remembered and treasured that moment
of gift and bliss at the hour of Vespers on the South Rim of
Yosemite, and only long thought and the discipline of these
written words has brought it out of eclipse and returned
it to me.

The Holy Spirit from time to time gives us moments of illumination, knowing that we need them. I need the illumination of the mountains and the ocean and the wild places, because there is so little in my daily life to remind me that the high-tech, cybernautical, and media-saturated bubble of virtual reality in which I live my life is just that — virtual, not real.

Have we enclosed ourselves so completely in the artifices of our own creativity that it takes a mountain or an ocean to bring us back to our senses? Are we so locked in the prison of our own bellowing desires and achievements and management strategies that we require a six-hour drive and a chill wind and high altitude and alpenglow just to bring to consciousness a moment of gratitude to God?

My honest answer to those questions is yes. I am no desert father. I am no saint. I am a thoroughly contemporary American Christian who struggles daily to maintain some kind of spiritual balance in the midst of a wired, nanosecond, jump-cut culture. Under the circumstances, it is tempting to blame "society" or "the media" or "modernity" for my difficulties. To do so would be a cooling salve for my wounded spiritual pride. But the problem is inside me, not outside me. The problem is my short spiritual memory and the fractured, dissipated, radically distracted state of my "normal" consciousness.

But in his wisdom and generosity, God made the mountains, and gave me eyes to gaze upon them. Even now I can lift my gaze from the flickering, unearthly illumination of an LCD monitor and see in mind's eye the alpenglow on the High Sierra. Even now I bring to mind the illumination of mountains and chill air and the evening sky filled with unseen angels, and for a moment, if I remember to make it so, my desk is an altar, my office a church. The beauty of the God who made the mountains emerges again from eclipse in my soul, and for a moment, I remember. Then I turn back to my tasks and my LCD monitor and all seems as it were — but somewhere in the mountains it is sunset, and I know that no one who has seen the light of God, if only for an instant, goes unchanged. Not even me.

Prayer on the Streets

ANNA B. OLSON

A priest learns to pray in the in-between places of her life.

THE TURN off Beverly and up Heliotrope is a visually harsh stretch. The lane of cars parked along a traffic island houses dealers and addicts. The usual hangers-on in the liquor store parking lot greet me with an enthusiastic "Hey lady!" and something between a leer and smile. Discarded mattresses interrupt the sidewalk, and the smell of urine rises from the pavement. But up ahead I can see the canopy of bougainvillea that marks a community garden reclaimed from a vacant lot, carefully tended by people from the neighborhood — a spot of beauty and sign of grace. I give thanks as I duck under the flowering vine's thorny branches, my eyes resting in the brilliance of its color.

Beyond the community garden, I cross the 101 Freeway from beneath. It's another sour spot, full of garbage and accumulated debris. Walking I see things that I never saw from the window of my car. Broken couches and old mattresses and discarded cardboard take shape overnight, forming small shelters. Just as quickly they are gone the next day — stolen, abandoned, removed by the city, I don't know. But they always reemerge, silent witnesses to tenacity and love of life even at the very margins of human existence.

I've learned to pray on the streets and buses and subways of the city of Los Angeles, in the in-between spaces of a crowded life as a parish priest, mother, spouse, activist. I pray with my eyes open, my feet moving on cracked pavement, with the sounds and smells of the city rising up to meet me.

I've always known this about myself: that my most alive moments in faith emerge in little spaces in the midst of chaos and action. But in recent years I betrayed this knowledge, spent far too much time trying to crowd my prayer life into proper silence and reverence at designated times, eyes closed, head bowed, holy words on my lips. The trouble was that there was no space in my life; the in-between had ceased to exist. Every minute had its purpose, neatly scheduled in a great juggle of child care, pastoral care, physical care of home, church, and body.

Only prayer refused to take its place on the agenda. It refused to show up when I made appointments for it in my calendar, refused to cry and demand attention like a neglected toddler, never flooded the parish hall as a visible reminder of deferred maintenance. All there was: a growing sense of distance, a cooling of relationship, a loss of intimacy.

So I left my car in the driveway and hit the streets.

I vowed to begin taking the time to travel from home to work on foot, to take public transportation to local meetings and appointments. I would learn the streets and the buses of my neighborhood. I began the project of reclaiming the in-between space. It's an imperfect discipline, complicated as is all my life by the urgencies of my various commitments. It's terribly inefficient in a city known for its slavish devotion to the automobile and corresponding neglect of public transit. It's hot and sweaty, grimy and slow. But I find that God meets me in the in-between spaces, multiplying my simple efforts, and it is more than worth it.

On my first bus trip from home to a diocesan meeting — a route I would come to know well — I headed off with careful directions gleaned from the transit authority Web site. As the bus meandered through neighborhoods and past schools, taking on mothers and strollers, letting off grand-mothers with their shopping and finally looping its way back toward the cathedral, I had more than my anticipated share of in-between time. The words of the prophet Isaiah came to me: "For my thoughts are not your thoughts, nor are your ways my ways, says the LORD. For as the heavens are higher than the earth, so are my ways higher than your ways and my thoughts than your thoughts." I don't know that the DASH bus schedule is nearly as high as the heavens, but the route was clearly planned with more than just my con-venience in mind. My car frees me to take routes meant only for me, to live without the inconvenience of planning

around other lives. On the bus I am but one member of the
larger body, one small piece of a picture too large for me to
comprehend.

Never is it more clear that we are all in this together
than when the bus breaks down and leaves us waiting twice
the scheduled amount of time. The minutes tick away. My
fellow travelers consult their watches, roll their eyes, shrug
their shoulders. I'm clearly not the only one who has somewhere to be, and a time to be there. But we're all stuck
together until the next bus comes. And the longer it takes
to get here, the less likely any of us will get to sit down. I
watch the drivers on the street, one to a car, battling their
own fears of lateness. They jockey for position, trying to
outdo one another, each hoping to arrive a little sooner.
I've been there a thousand times, will be there again. But
today I'd rather be at the bus stop, where no amount of
elbowing or jostling will get me there any sooner than any
of my sisters or my brothers.

When I was ordained a priest, my bishop read to me from
the Book of Common Prayer: "My sister, in all that you do,
you are to nourish Christ's people from the riches of his
grace, and strengthen them to glorify God in this life and
in the life to come." In the short span of my ordained life I
have tried far too often to nourish myself and others from
the shallow pool of my own resources, ignoring entirely the
riches of God's grace. I usually can't quite bring myself to
believe in the sufficiency of grace. In the in-between times

of walking and waiting, I begin to see a lesson in grace. In my car, I create my own movement, just me and internal combustion and fossil fuel. It's easy and efficient. But the bus passes whether I'm on it or not. In the muscles of my legs and the passing of the bus I have found the deeper pool, the richness of resource that is there and ready to move me on my way, less efficient in the short term, but sustainable in a way that my just-for-me plan will never be.

My bus project has generated a fair amount of interest. I hear again and again, "Nobody walks and takes the bus in L.A." Actually lots of people do. The buses are often full, and the sidewalks of my neighborhood are never empty. More precisely, virtually nobody who's white and educated and middle class and owns a home takes the bus. There is an element of class treason in this project, noted both by my socioeconomic peers and my fellow bus riders. When I run into my working-class parishioners on the bus, they look worried. "Are you all right? Did something happen to your car?" More than once a kind fellow bus rider has asked if I know where I'm going or if I need directions — not normal bus behavior, just one more sign that they look at me and know I don't belong. Riding the bus in L.A. is not a spiritual experience for most people. The buses are slow and irregular. They rarely follow the most efficient route from point to point. Add a stroller, small children, a bag of groceries, a tightly scheduled appointment, and the bus quickly becomes a misery. The puzzled concern on my parishioners' faces in part reflects the reality that, with a car in the driveway, there's no way you'd find them on the bus.

None of my great discoveries on the bus and the street are new in Christian tradition. Intention matters. A small effort on my part to open space for prayer brings more than equal effort on God's part. Prayer in light of the incarnation is about opening my eyes, not closing them, letting the world in, not shutting it out. God is everywhere. My fellow human beings are precious and beautiful in their struggles to survive and move around this city.

One day I am walking home from work when it begins to rain. I get wetter and wetter. By the time I get to the main street, I am dripping enough to be too embarrassed to duck into any of the small variety stores in hopes of finding an umbrella for sale. How could a predictable winter rain have caught me so completely off guard? Without the bubble of my car to insulate me, I am more than a quick building-to-building dash from dryness. Shocked to discover my belief that I was impervious to changes in the weather, I muddle on toward home feeling ridiculous and human, deeply aware of the squelch of my shoes, the sky overhead, bare skin in direct contact with creation.

At the corner of Beverly and Union, I find myself temporarily stranded when the DASH bus fails to arrive. A handful of people gather, waiting. A boy in baggy pants, skipping school, not more than fourteen or fifteen, asks an older woman for a dime to complete the twenty-five-cent fare. He asks in Spanish, politely. She shakes her head, careful not to speak or meet his eyes, moves away. He asks me too, and I dig a dime out of my wallet. A police car passes looking for truants, and he ducks out of sight. I ask the older woman how long she has been waiting for the bus. When she discovers I speak Spanish, she moves closer, confessing the truth of her refusal to share a dime. "I'm afraid of them," she said, nodding her head in the direction of the boy. "You never know what they'll do — assault you or just grab your purse and run." Them — all the baggy-pants-wearing, school-skipping, could-be-gangsters, bus-riding boys. I hear her word of caution to me, and I don't doubt her warning comes from lived experience. I pray for a world where we have come to fear our own children, for teenagers growing up seeing fear and their own reflections mixed in the eyes of their grandmothers.

Beverly Boulevard is lined with tiny storefronts promising secure shipping to Guatemala, Honduras, El Salvador. When it's shipping day, the curb fills with packages, ready to be loaded into a waiting truck. These are large items, mostly electronics — washers and dryers, stoves, microwaves, and televisions. I watch the fruits of working-class wages begin their trek south to fulfill promises to those left behind. I know that the immigrant parishioners in my multiethnic parish, almost to a person, set aside a significant share of already tight budgets to send money and gifts to family at home. It is a glimpse into a world that I do not inhabit. There is no one waiting for me to send their monthly allowance, to make the difference between starvation and subsistence, or even to add the finishing touch of a big-screen TV or washer-dryer combo. I confess one God, maker of heaven and earth, in whom we live and move and have our being. That God somehow inhabits and links both our worlds. We are not so separate as we might imagine, I and those washing machines on the curb, and those who will receive them.

Los Angeles has a subway, after a fashion. It's not the sort of get-you-where-you-want-to-go system that New York has, but if you happen to be going where it's going, it's a treat. The stations are cool and high-ceilinged, each one designed with some quirky L.A.-related theme. The trains run reasonably often, and the platforms offer the perfect space for walking meditation. I walk slowly from one end of the platform to the other, counting my steps or letting my thoughts collect around a simple verse or phrase. Unlike waiting for the bus, which will roar right on by the unwary, waiting for the train requires no attention whatsoever. When the train does come, a rush of wind and gradual escalation of sound eases me out of my meditation. There is plenty of time to board.

Each time I manage a whole day on public transit, making the stops I need to make, executing transfers, getting my money's worth on the three-dollar day pass, I feel a little lighter. My legs may ache from climbing the broken escalators of the subway station, or my breath strain from running to make a connection, but I feel a lightness in the touch of my feet on the ground, a lightness in my own living on the face of God's creation. Each time I leave my car and move my muscles and hop the bus or train, I can feel the weight of my footprint on the earth, easing just a little, the creation breathing just a little easier. I cannot say that I was aware of the heaviness, but it must have been there, for I can feel it lifting.

Listening

KAY LINDAHL

A spirituality workshop leader and author
highlights the prayerful qualities of listening.

THE PAST one hundred years have brought us amazing advances in technology. We have gone from the first airplane flight at Kitty Hawk in 1903 to supersonic jets, space travel, and explorations of the planets. Communication that used to take weeks or months to reach its destination is now received almost instantaneously. We live in the Information Age, where we are inundated with words, data, news. Even though we have mastered much in the physical world, the world of technology, we still haven't learned how to treat each other. All we have to do is read the news, or turn on the TV or radio.

In times like these, our most important work must be in the intangible world — the world of communication, relationships, loving each other.

The capacity to listen is one of the keys to this work. We have paid a great deal of attention to learning how to speak, and very little to learning how to listen. Think of the difference it would make if each of us really felt heard

239

when we spoke. Imagine the time it would save to be heard the first time around, instead of having to repeat ourselves over and over again. Envision a conversation where each person is listened to with respect, even those whose views are different from ours. It takes intention and commitment. We need to slow down to expand our awareness of the possibilities of deep listening. The simple act of listening to each other can transform all of our relationships. Indeed, it can transform the world as we practice being the change we wish to see in the world.

We can focus on some practices that prepare us for this experience by engaging with three foundational qualities of listening: *silence, reflection,* and *presence.*

Anyone who wants to be good at something practices. We need to exercise our listening muscles, and we do that by practicing. As we practice we begin to notice how these concepts relate to all areas of our lives. They are about being, not doing. We become a listening presence.

There's a Cuban proverb that says, *"Listening looks easy, but it's not simple. Every head is a world."*

◆ ◆ ◆

The following story illustrates how these practices impacted a personal relationship. It happened on the most micro level, with my husband, and yet I think the principles apply all the way up to the most macro level.

A few years ago we experienced water damage in our house. It was determined that we needed to replace all the carpeting. I love wooden floors, so I thought that this would be the perfect time to make that change. My husband was totally against this idea, which really surprised me, as he'd grown up in the Midwest where wooden floors were the norm. His reasons didn't make sense to me, and I really wanted the wooden floors, so I was ready to draw a line in the sand on this one.

One day, after my daily practice of *silent meditation*, it occurred to me that there was more to his story, and I needed to listen to my husband one more time. I didn't want to do this, I just knew that I had to. So then I *reflected* and asked myself what question wanted to be asked. What came to me was that I had asked why he didn't want wooden floors and got reasons that sounded unreasonable to me. This time I asked him what it was about wooden floors that bothered him. In order to be *fully present* to him I let go of my agenda and was genuinely curious about what he would say. What I found out was that it was the fact that we have a concrete slab underflooring and putting wood on concrete was completely out of integrity for him, as an architect, as he views wood as a structural material. In an instant I was able to let go of my insistence on wooden floors because I finally understood what was behind his resistance. It was easy to put myself in his shoes and see how much it would grate on his sensitivity each time he walked on the floor.

◆ ◆ ◆

Cultivating *silence* is about listening to the silence, listening beyond words. It is also called contemplative listening. It's about taking time to be quiet and simply be. We are so busy running around doing things. This *practice* is to stop doing for a moment, be quiet, and listen. There can be no listening without silence. A daily practice of silence leads to a closer relationship to God; it's about listening to God.

The next *practice* is slowing down to *reflect*. Reflective listening is listening to yourself—your True Self—getting to know the voice of your soul. In deepening our relationship to ourselves, we develop the sensitivity to listen to our own inner voice. Once we learn to know and trust this voice, we find ourselves moving from inner peace to outer action with ease.

How do we get to know this inner voice? It's a practice of listening for the questions. Take a few breaths before responding to a situation, question, or comment. Ask yourself what wants to be said next. Not what do I want to say (the ego) but what wants to be said (from the soul). Wait for your inner voice to respond. Listen for your true wisdom to reveal itself. We are so used to being in our heads, our minds, our intellect, it may take awhile for our inner voice to appear. It's a slowing down, waiting, practicing patience.

Being present, listening from the heart, listening which connects us, is the *third practice* that supports the sacred art of listening. An exercise to support being present is to take a minute or two each day to be fully aware of everything that is happening during that time. Most of us are so used to multitasking that it seems strange to focus on just what's happening in the moment.

Deep listening occurs at the heart level. It is present when we feel most connected to another person or to a group of people. Our hearts expand, and our capacity to communicate with those of differing beliefs and customs increases. It is also about hospitality: offering space where change can take place, where there's a freedom to be. It's being fully present with another. I call this heart listening.

◆ ◆ ◆

Really listening to one another is one of the greatest gifts we have to give. It requires our full attention. It calls for a mind-set of appreciation, curiosity, wonder for the other person. We can't be thinking about what we are going to say in response or how we would handle the situation. It is communicating from the heart. It takes practice to be able to let go of our own agendas to be present with another.

For me, listening is really about opening up to love. David Augsberger says it so well: *"Being listened to is so close to being loved that most people cannot tell the difference."*

Listening takes time, intention, and commitment. It is a sacred act.

T-Cells and Empathy

MARK THOMPSON

A seasoned therapist and author makes prayer real...
with the help of two remarkable friends.

*E*VERY WEDNESDAY at four o'clock, Patti Motogawa and
I walked home from school together. We must have
been quite a sight, but we didn't care. She in heavy metal leg
braces scraping the pitted concrete. Me tagging along with
two shiny black violin cases conspicuously balanced. Patti
was always impeccably dressed, a large white handkerchief
in hand to mop the constant beads of saliva on her lip. I
opted for a canary yellow double-breasted sweater on those
special days.

The other kids didn't want much to do with either one
of us, but we were special friends. We certainly had the
bonds of music in common — first and second chair in our
school's youth symphony orchestra — but also that secret
pact of the heart that comes from being labeled outsiders.

Patti was inflicted with a crippling childhood disease:
polio, I believe, although no one was supposed to say it. As
a result, her gait was painfully encumbered and her speech

almost indiscernible. But her parents, proud Japanese Americans who met while interred at the Manzanar relocation camp during World War II, had well endowed Patti with their gift of self-esteem.

I was on more shaky ground when it came to self-confidence; the violin apparently signaled to my peers that there was an incipient sissy in their midst. But none of this mattered with Patti, especially after midweek practice when I escorted her home. For I was never more gallant and she never more beautiful than during the long walk up Hillcrest Avenue, intimate in our laughter as the first wisps of fog began their nightly embrace of our small coastal community.

It was 1962, and we were both about ten years old. The age of our innocence — and the nation's — was soon to end. Yet in all the decades that have followed, and life's vicissitudes endured, I have never forgotten the simple lesson that Patti's friendship offered. For many, there could be no greater hardship than the one she was dealt. But somehow Patti made her burdens light. When she played the violin it was about so much more than keeping the notes on key. Her music enveloped you, inviting you along into her own private joy.

One day, I asked Patti what inspired her to create such exquisite tones, in contrast to my own dutiful but often scratchy sawing. In the heavy, slurred sounds she could barely muster, Patti replied that she sometimes asked for help. "But where?" I naively wondered. At this point, my friend said nothing, only gesturing upward with a flick of her crisp linen.

Not long after this, my family moved to another town, and I never saw Patti again. But her unhesitant reference to another place, beyond the one we mundanely inhabit, never left me. *So, that's what some people do when they want to ask for strength, or help, or just consolation,* I began to reason. As to where, I had no idea. But the *how* of it became ever more clear. I don't imagine that Patti would have used the word "prayer," but I am certain that's what she meant. While I grew up obediently bowing my head in Sunday school, she is the first person I met who didn't pray without thinking, who meant it as a conscious act of communication. The reason *why* some people pray as Patti did — and I do today — is now obvious.

I began to pray in earnest about twenty years after my conversation that day on the sidewalk, when many other friends became stricken, then disabled, then deceased, from a virus as seemingly mysterious and awesome as the one that had afflicted Patti. There was no cure, or containment, or even much sympathy in sight. What else could one do in the face of such dreadful assault — other than to tend the dying, and take grievance to the streets — but to pray? The day I found out I had AIDS, too, about half my lifetime ago, I walked out into a garden and prayed for myself.

Never have I felt less self-pitying and more self-empowered than by claiming that simple act. Were the gods, a God, or even "Miss God," as the poet W. H. Auden archly put it, waiting and watching? That all seemed much less important than lowering a bucket of conscious intent into my own deep well of faith and personal meaning. I wasn't asking to be saved or to avoid suffering (because I believe prayer doesn't quite work that way), but rather to be fully awakened with acceptance and grace to the challenges ahead.

Once I allowed the importance of prayer, I had to decide what to do with it. After all, there seems to be a kind of hierarchy of prayerful wishes always circulating in our lives — from the unintentionally trivial ("Best regards! I'll keep you in my thoughts and prayers.") to the overly somber ("Now, sinners, let us get down on our knees and pray."). Neither approach was particularly meaningful to me. Instead, I had to find out for myself *how* prayer works and then employ it on that level.

The best explanation about the practical application of prayer was given to me by a very wise person I've been lucky to know most of my life. We met when one of my best pals in high school took me home for lunch. I took an immediate liking to this warm and gracious woman, her mother. And over the years, through adolescence and well into adulthood, we've enjoyed an ever-evolving friendship. A lifelong Roman Catholic, Laurette's belief is often tested when her liberal views clash with church dogma. Yet she maintains both principles and her faith. This deep resolve comes from

actively praying for things that she feels passionate about —
including me.

"I prayed today for your T-cells to go up," Laurette has
often told me. Finally, one day, I expressed curiosity about
how the process of prayer actually works for her — and,
apparently, both of us. After years of being parked in a very
low place, my T-cells were at last taking off in the opposite
direction. I could attribute the change to wondrous new
chemicals, but somehow I thought there was more to it
than science alone.

My friend responded by telling me a story about a mad-
cap heiress she had once known. A life-of-every-party type,
who'd been told by doctors she could no longer party, Laurette's acquaintance was determined to make one last gala.
Feverish with cancer, she barely stumbled into a waiting
ambulance, despite the pleading of attendants. But when
she got to the glittering soiree, something miraculous had
occurred. The fever was gone, and the lady was ready for
one last ball. When asked how this happened, the woman
replied that she'd imagined a thermometer in her head and
willed the fever to go down inch by inch.

"So, when I pray for you," said Laurette, "I, too, imagine
a big thermometer filled with your T-cells and invite them
to go up." Knowing that Laurette consistently prays for me
has bolstered my own belief in the power of active prayer.
I have said many prayers for the dead (it's how I keep alive
memories of those I've loved and lost), and for life itself. But

here, in one short conversation, a generality was made specific — and all the more real. A vague hunch was instantly clarified into a workable practice.

It's not enough to ask that "things get better" or that "someone come and help me," but rather to state *how*, and *when*, and *why*. In 2003, about fourteen thousand people a day were infected with HIV, adding to the over 40 million people already infected globally, and the 20 million plus now dead. When I pray about AIDS, I am requesting not only my own recovery, but the recovery of sanity in leaders who preach denial instead of enlightened measures, intolerance over hope. I pray for a thousand fewer people each day to wake up and find themselves — and their families — afflicted with humankind's deadliest disease ever.

Laurette and I now make a kind of team when it comes to our prayers about AIDS. An effort made by two, that has all the room in the world to encompass others, much like those pictures of skydivers linking hands to create a giant web in the sky. It takes many people to make a difference, in prayer life as in any other worthwhile and lasting endeavor.

I remember the first time I witnessed how the concerted devotion of many can make a difference to just a single one. It was a brisk October afternoon in Pacific Grove, during a celebration of the Monarch Butterflies' annual return. These fragile creatures migrate over twenty-five hundred miles each year from Alaska to warmer habitats on California's central coast. Arriving in enormous swarms, they paint the skies and their ancestral groves with swathes of brilliant orange.

The town's schoolchildren dress up as big butterflies and march down Main Street, papier-mâché wings fluttering in an ocean breeze always festooned with countless Monarchs. A high point of the festivities is the passing of the parade's anointed Queen, seated on a throne while pulled along on a giant wagon.

And, so, there was Patti, my fellow violinist, triumphantly aloft. Serenaded by the music of loving cheers, radiant in a cloud of iridescent butterflies. She was blessed that day with a prayer of ten thousand wings.

The Seasons Tumble

Harvey Cox

*An acclaimed author, thinker, and educator
drifts a bit — ecumenically — when he prays.*

Part I: Personal Prayer

I pray more now than I used to. I do not think it is aging.
I think it is that I have learned different ways to pray and
have found that praying is a vital ingredient in my life.

I am sure some will find my pattern of prayer unduly
syncretistic, if not chaotic. Let me say, however, that I prefer
to call it ecumenical, and that this reflects who I am as a
would-be Christian.

I begin with my personal prayers, so let's start in the
morning. Even though I remain a (somewhat uncomfortable) Baptist, I cross myself as soon as I wake up, before I
get out of bed, and thank God that I have been gifted with
another day of life. After I wash and dress, I read a few
words of something. This varies widely. I have turned to a
little book of thought and prayers by Jewish mystics; *Letters
to Young Churches* (a modern translation of the Epistles);
the Gospels; a prayer from the good old Episcopal Book

of Common Prayer; Thomas Merton's *Thoughts in Solitude;*
The Wisdom of the Prophet: Sayings of Muhammad; Catherine
Whitmire's *Plain Living: A Quaker Path to Simplicity.* I have
used others, but this conveys the idea.

I do not read for long. Only a few verses, a couple
paragraphs.

As I read, I stand by my window, looking out on the
corner of Frost and Prentiss streets in Cambridge, Massachusetts. The seasons tumble by. Leaves turn to red and
gold. It rains. Snow falls, sometimes lots and lots of snow.
It rains again. Spring eventually comes. Tiny green buds
appear. Then summer, full-leafed on the maple trees, ar-
rives. Then autumn, my favorite season in New England,
returns again.

After I close the book, I put a CD on my bedside player.
I prefer Gregorian Chant, but have used Black gospel. Ma-
halia Jackson does get one going on a sluggish morning. I
then turn to a tiny wooden Orthodox icon of Christ I once
brought back from Russia. Then I start my short prayer.
While the music plays I cross myself again. I go through
phases with this. Sometimes I do it "Western," but, especially when I have been traveling in Orthodox lands,
sometimes in "Eastern" style. I then thank God, again, for
life and this new day. Then I follow a kind of routine. I pray
for a different one of my four children and (for the married
ones) for their spouses and children on each successive day.
Every Friday I pray for my wife Nina. It seems right to do

that on Friday since it is the beginning of Sabbath and she is Jewish. Then, again somewhat systematically, I thank God each day for one of my five senses, beginning with my eyes on Monday, and so on. This also helps me to remember to take care of those senses and to be more aware of what I am seeing, tasting, smelling, hearing, touching. I always say some prayer (they vary) for someone I know in need, and for the poor and mistreated wherever they are. Then I use a large, round, full-arm gesture, almost the way Pentecostals pray, and "turn this day over" to God. That is something I learned in a Twelve-Step program many years ago.

Our corner is not a quiet one. Cars and trucks zoom through the intersection as I read and pray. People walk by in shorts or light jackets or heavy parkas, depending on the season. Children make their way to school. Dogs trot by. I do not consider any of this to be a distraction. I sometimes thank God for them and try to intercede for them, although I usually don't know what kind of intercession they need. (We rarely do.) Now I am ready for breakfast!

As I leave the house, I touch the mezuzah tacked to our door frame. It contains a small portion of the Torah, but my gesture is another thank-you to God for my home. When I arrive at my office, I thank God for the opportunity to work, teach, write. As I do I face a Mexican tile panel with a simple depiction of Our Lady of Guadalupe on it. Next to it stands a small, framed set of two Arabic words from the

Qur'an, given to me by a student. They are the words for
"insight" and "wisdom."

Part II: Corporate Prayer

I do not believe the Christian life can be a solo flight. So, of
course, my praying also expresses itself in corporate settings
as well as in the "closet."

I have never found a perfect church, so I tend to drift
a bit. At present I attend St. James Episcopal Church near
my home. It is of the broad/low variety. I thrive on the symbolic and sacramental elements. Communion for me, with
its stately traditional prayers, with everyone of all shapes
coming to the altar rail, is a prefiguring of the ultimate gathering of the whole human family without respect to rank.
St. James also has the most ethnically diverse, racially het-
erogeneous, and mixed-age congregation I know of in the
Boston area. It anticipates what the kingdom of God will be
like. I am there every Sunday that I am in town.

Home prayers with my little family of three (the three
older kids are married) also count as corporate. We always begin our evening meal with the prayer, "Baruch atah
adonai, eloheinu melech ha'olam, ha motzi lechem min
ha'aretz" (yes, we say it together in Hebrew!), thanking God
who "brings forth bread from the earth." On the death date
of someone, we light candles and say the Kaddish.

Every Friday when we gather for supper we light the Sabbath candles, intone the traditional Hebrew prayers over the lights (said by the mother), the wine (said by me), and the bread (said by Nicholas, our son). I treasure this Sabbath ritual more than I can say. Often my married son and his two children join us, frequently other friends and relatives. I know the earliest Christians continued to celebrate the Sabbath. I wish we all still did.

On "high holidays" — both Jewish and Christian — we pray the traditional prayers and sing the traditional songs. That includes Passover, Hanukah, Thanksgiving, Christmas, and Easter, which we sometimes celebrate at home on the Orthodox date since my wife's parents came from Russia and the tradition remains alive. That is also why we all sit together just before we leave for a trip to say the "Spogum" prayer, a Russian blessing for safe return.

Once or twice a year I sneak off to a Benedictine monastery in Hingham, Massachusetts (Glastonbury Abbey), for two days of prayer, rest, jogging, attendance at the offices, and (a little) reading. I usually walk/pray through the Stations of the Cross while I am there.

As I look back over this essay, it sounds like a LOT of praying. It does not feel that way to me. Prayer is not an add-on anymore. It is woven into my daily, monthly, annual pattern. Maybe that is what the Apostle meant when he said, "Pray without ceasing"?